Goosberry Jam

1 seer goosberry, add one seer suga
if you intend to keeping it for a
long time. But 6 chts is suffecent
boil together with a piece of
cinnamon, until the syrup is q
thick.   *very good*

Guava Marmalade

Strain the pulp of the 100 guavers throu
a piece of net, add one seer or a little
more sugar according to taste add a
wine-glass of lime juice cook over a
fire stirring all the while, till the
juice dries.   *very good*

Guava Jelly.

100 guavers cut into slices put as mu
water as will cover it boil on a bris

A page from one of the original recipe books written by Bill Lethorn's Grandmother circa 1900

THE HOPE FOUNDATION

ANGLO INDIAN RECIPES & REMEDIES

A LEGACY OF MUCH LOVED FAMILY RECIPES

BILL LETHORN

Published by Lethorn Publishing 2016
29 Claremont Park, Finchley, London, N3 1TG

© Mark Carey: Hope Foundation photography
© Tony Briscoe: recipe photography
© William Lethorn: archive family photos

Available mail order and from selected book sellers
Sales and enquiries: info@thehopefoundation.org.uk

Printed in England by Russell Press Ltd.
ISBN Number: 978-0-9558003-1-3

CONTENTS

INTRODUCTION

Bill Lethorne

Recently amongst all the papers in my archives, I found hand-written recipes and remedies in pencil which had started to fade. These wonderful pages instantly conjured up the sensory memories of taste and smell of the food my grandmother cooked in Calcutta. The majority of these hand-written gems must have been written in the late 1800's or early 1900's by my grandmother. My family lived mainly in Cossipore, the jute refinery of Calcutta (Kolkata) from the late 1800's. This was the time of the British Raj when the Anglo Indian Mother, or Mam-sahib reigned supreme in the home. The Mem-sahib did not do any housework, she gave orders and made sure that they were correctly carried out and whilst she controlled the recipes, the domestic help controlled the culinary magic, the alchemy that bought the recipes to life.

I have not adjusted any recipes for the purpose of this book, any items which I thought needed some additional explanation I have marked with an asterisk and explained in the glossary. Certain recipes contain the word Bindaloo which is now known as Vindaloo. In India Bindaloo was made either hot or mild to taste and not hot only, as in the majority of restaurants now outside of India. Karti Kebab was a very special dish which I loved, usually eaten with parathas and I am surprised that this dish is not found more often in more Indian restaurants.

The Anglo Indian Mam-sahib usually catered for a large family or did one large preparation a year to make chutneys or the like, hence a recipe may start with 'take 100 mangoes (guavas)'. The Milk Punch recipe is especially interesting "3 bottles of rum....". Try it and then forget about life for a bit. The recipes in this book remind me of the magic of the India that I love, of my childhood and the intrinsic link between our cultures.

Taken in Kodamah, Bihar circa 1900. My Grandmother, seated wrote most of the recipes in this book and my Mother who also wrote some of the recipes is the girl on her left

Also taken in Kodamah circa 1915. My Grandmother is seated and Grandfather is standing to her left

Anglo Indian family at play, taken at the family premises in Cosipore, Kolkata circa 1910. Grandmother is in the middle row, second from the right and Mother is seated on her left

FOREWORD

Maureen Forrest, Founder of The Hope Foundation

Education is the best passport out of poverty, but no child can learn on an empty stomach. Amongst the work of The Hope Foundation in Kolkata, one of the greatest gifts that is offered is that of positive nutrition. As food forms the centre of family life around the world and particularly in India, and West Bengal, thousands of children and their parents amble through daily life without knowing where their next meal will come from. The Hope Foundation, through the generosity of individuals, continues to reach out to thousands of children on a daily basis, offering protection, healthcare, nutrition, counselling and a future. As you wind your way through the many recipes in this book, please keep in mind those who are not as fortunate as those of us who have a regular supply of food and shelter. Please do enjoy the read, it is a truly wonderful glimpse into the culinary past of Calcutta, supporting The Hope Foundation.

Maureen Forrest has dedicated her life to protecting some of the world's most vulnerable and disadvantaged children by founding The Hope Foundation in 1999. She has made a very real and positive impact on the lives of hundreds of thousands of children, many of whom would not be alive today without her help. Maureen believes in creating sustainable solutions to the issues and problems associated with poverty, and has a holistic approach to healing lives. She is deeply committed to getting as many children into education as possible. Since its beginnings, The Hope Foundation has positively affected 2.3 million people and will continue to be there for the vulnerable children of Kolkata, and their families, for as long as they need help. Maureen strives to protect children and address the underlying causes of the daily struggles faced by those living on the streets.

FROM OUR SPONSOR

Arun Kapil, Green Saffron Spices Ltd.

I'm thrilled to be a small part of Bill's book and to have a proud association with The Hope Foundation. This a beautiful tome, diligently curated for an excellent cause. I started my spice company, Green Saffron in Midleton, Co Cork, Ireland in 2007 with my Irish wife, Olive. We bring fresh, new season spice out of India, trading direct with farmers and local 'mundis' (markets). Our origins lie in India, rooted in the UK, we're at home in Ireland, so it wasn't too long before we linked-up with neighbours Maureen and Susan Forrest to produce a sachet mix of spice donating profits of its sale to Hope. The Hope Foundation is very much a forward thinking, deeply caring organisation and we're immensely proud that through their fantastic efforts we're able to help support street children in Kolkata. This book is testament to their unerring commitment to 'a world where it should never hurt to be a child' and I wish it only the absolute best. Shukriya.

Spice is one of the oldest traded commodities. Levants to the Romans, Portugese to Elizabethan English and Dutch, so many trading nations have brought these exotic fruits, seeds, barks, roots, husks and leaves to the forefront of global cuisine. At Green Saffron, we strive to go one step further than convention focussing on the freshest, most vibrant, highest grade spice. We're a family of spice traders and great home cooks. We understand our ingredients from responsible farm to discerning fork. Just like great vineyards and cocoa plantations, great spices come from great farms. We've developed our own fully traceable, fully sustainable fresh spice route. We have family boots-on-ground to guarantee a fully robust, 100% trustworthy chain from source to sauce, but we mainly just want to bring you the best in the most accessible way we can.

Slow Roast 'Kolkata' Beef Rib-eye, Curried Bones, Chilli Crumb

Root Vegetable & Onion Pakoras, Pineapple Piccalilli,
Dressed Cottage Cheese.
Serves 6 to 8.

I created this recipe for Bill's book with a foot fixed firmly in both camps –
Britain and India. I'm an Anglo Indian – Dad was born a Hindu in north India,
Mum's Yorkshire born and bred – so I've been a mix from the get go.
My day-to-day life as a 'Spiceman' happily revolves around trading fresh
spice from farms, creating blends, recipes and building my brand, Green
Saffron. Much in the same way Bill's book opens a window on his family's
cooking, this recipe is a celebration of my upbringing. I have taken a
beautiful cut of beef as the centre piece, added a dash of subtle spicing and
many recognisable Indian elements to enhance and adorn the dish.

I've taken East Indian warming spices and based this recipe on a typical
Kolkata dish. It's my nod to modern British Indian cooking, starring an
indulgent cut of beef, embellishing with typical Eastern flair. The marrow
bones play an important part in the eating, bringing richness to the sauce
so do try to get some from your butcher. All told, it's quite a mammoth 4
recipes in 1, however, you can simply make the rib roast without all my
suggested trimmings opting instead for roast potatoes and carrots,
but do try 'the works' when you've got the time.

Beef Rib-eye

Ingredients

2kg of a 2 bone
   rib-eye joint on
   the bone,
   28 -35 days dry aged
90ml sunflower oil
2 packets of Green
   Saffron Kolkata
   Chaap Spice Mix
   or a mix of:
2 tbsb garam masala
1tbsp fresh ground
   black pepper
   nutmeg grated
5 cloves fresh ground
1 tsp Kashmiri chilli
   flakes
2 tsp sea salt
2 brown onions diced
6 cloves garlic grated
25g root ginger grated
70g cashew nuts
240g natural yoghurt
300ml hot water
3 or 4 beef marrow
   bones cut 15cm long
   lengthwise

Finishing:
1 tblsp rose water or
   the zest of 1 lime
Fresh mint and
   coriander chopped
20g best quality
pistachio nuts, unsalted,
peeled and lightly
cracked

Method

Place the rib joint onto a large plate, pour over
half the oil and half the spice blend, massage
well, cover loosely with cling-film and set aside
for 1 hour. Take a casserole dish, pour in the
remaining oil, add the onions and fry for about 8
to 10 minutes until they become soft, then add the
garlic, ginger and sugar.

Remove from the heat. Pop this fried onion
mixture, the nuts, yoghurt, remaining spice blend
into a food processor and blitz to a smooth paste.
Set aside.

Turn your oven to 180°C, gas mark 4. Take a
5-6cm high sided cast iron roasting tray, pop it
onto a high heat, when scorching hot add
the beef and sear all sides, then remove the tray
from the heat. Pour the spiced mixture around the
seared beef joint, add the hot water, cover with
foil and pop into your oven on a middle shelf.

Roast for about 2 to 2 and half hours, or until
the rib's core temperature is 50°C, then add
the 3 or 4 marrow bones around the beef joint,
cover again with the foil and roast for another 15
minutes or until the core temperature is 55°C to
59°C. Remove from the oven, rest the meat in the
tray loosely covered with the foil.

Chilli Crumb

Ingredients

Method

150g breadcrumbs
1 red finger chilli
1 small onion
Zest of lemon
2 cloves garlic
Handful parsley
1-2 tblsp light oil

Finely dice all the dry ingredients. In a small bowl, mix with the other ingredients, adding the oil little by little until all the mixture becomes only just coated, then lightly toast in a dry fry pan. Set aside.

Pakora

Ingredients

Method

2 brown onions sliced
400g mix diced
   carrots & parsnips
300g gram flour
1 tbsp sunflower oil
Handful coriander
1 tbsp mustard seeds
1 tsp turmeric
1 tsp salt
Juice & zest lime
Oil for deep frying

Heat the oil to 170°C. Add all the ingredients and just enough water to mix and bind them together, forming a thick batter.

Drop tablespoon batches of the batter into the hot oil and cook until golden brown all over, about 5 minutes. Set aside on kitchen paper.

Pineapple Piccalilli

Ingredients

Method

2 red onions diced
5 shallots sliced
2 red chillies sliced
1 green chilli sliced
1 tsp sea salt
2 tbsp mustard oil
Spice:
2 tsp fresh ground black
pepper, 7 cloves
3 tsp tumeric, ½ fresh
   nutmeg grated

Pop the onion, shallot quarters and chillies into a bowl, sprinkle with the salt and set aside for about 45 minutes.

In a large pot, heat the oil, then add the black pepper, cloves and stir for a minute, then, stirring all the time add the turmeric, nutmeg, mustard powder, flour and 50ml of the vinegar to form a thick paste.

1 tbsp mustard powder
2 tbsp plain flour
250ml cider vinegar
2 eating apples, peeled and grated
1 medium pineapple, cored, peeled and diced into 25mm chunks. You can use 2 cans (approx. 850g) of pineapple chunks, just drain and dice the slices first
3 tbsp sugar

Then add the remaining vinegar, cook gently for about 5 minutes adding a little water as you go, so to form a smooth viscous paste of coating consistency.

Add the apple, pineapple, sugar and continue to cook for 2 minutes. Rinse and drain the salted ingredients, add them to the pot, keep stirring from time to time and cook gently until the onions just begin to soften.

Set aside to use later or to store, spoon straight away into sterilised jar(s) and seal. This will keep for up to a month in the fridge.

Dressed Cottage Cheese

Ingredients

Method

300g natural, full fat cottage cheese
Small handful coriander leaves, finely chopped
1 tsp toasted cumin seeds
Squeeze of lemon juice

Mix all ingredients together in a small bowl, then pop into your fridge until you're ready to serve.

To serve

- Remove the meat joint from the roasting tray
- Finish the 'Chaap' sauce, removing and discarding the now empty 15cm bones, then whisking in the rose water and herbs over a gentle heat to make an unctuous sauce
- Warm the Pakoras and crumb in the oven
- Carefully carve down the 2 rib bones, discard the bones, then slice generously the rested joint onto a warmed charger, coat with the Chaap sauce, sprinkle with the crumb then cracked pistachios
- Warmed serving bowl of Pakoras piled high, the piccalilli and cottage cheese in smaller unheated dishes by the side. Enjoy!

PUBLISHER'S NOTE

This is very much a heritage cookbook and should be regarded in that light. It is a charming collection of recipes taken from William (Bill) Lethorn's personal archives which have been typed up exactly as they appear in his grandmother's and mother's handwritten exercise books.

The recipes were written over the course of 100 years and as a result, have varying methods of cooking (fire, stove, oven), inconsistent temperatures (centigrade and gas) and a wide variety of measures dating back to the complex weights and measures system of colonial times (many explained in the glossary). Where no exact ingredients are given, this is because they were not included in the original, have faded and are illegible, or the well-thumbed pages have torn and disintegrated over time. Whilst some recipes have detailed instructions, others have been written with the assumption of a certain level of culinary knowledge and experience, and the instructions are brief, verging on non-existent.

The book includes many delicious recipes which we hope you will take inspiration from to build your own legacy of family favourites, which can be passed down the generations. Due to the sheer number of recipes, we have not been able to try out each and every one, so you may well have to use your own imagination, interpretation and some flexibility to achieve perfect results!

SNACKS &
SAVOURIES

Cheese Puffs

Ingredients

2 oz flour
2 oz potatoes
1½ oz butter
¼ tsp each salt &
    pepper
Eggs to bind
Rolled oats
½ tsp baking
    powder
2 oz grated cheese

Method

Mix flour, baking powder and potatoes together. Rub in butter. Add cheese and seasoning. Bind with eggs.

Roll out and cut into fingers or rounds. Coat with egg and toss in rolled oats. Bake in a moderate oven for 20 minutes.

Cheese Fritters

Ingredients

½ pint cold water
½ ounce butter
½ yolk of egg
1 egg white
¼ tsp of baking
    powder
2 oz flour
½ oz of grated
    cheese
Salt and mustard to
taste

Method

Put water and butter in a saucepan. Sift flour with salt and mustard and add to water and butter when comes to a boil. Stir well on the fire till the mixture is quite smooth and leaves the sides of the saucepan.

When cool beat in the baking powder, cheese and egg yolk. Then stir in the whites stiffly frothed. Drop teaspoonfuls of the mixture into smoking hot fat.

Fry till crisp and golden. Drain on paper and serve hot.

Salted Almonds

Ingredients

2 lbs of almonds
1 tbsp salad oil
1 tsp salt

Method

Blanch about 2 lbs of almonds and pour
over them a tablespoon of salad oil.
Let them stand in this for a couple of
hours. Then add a teaspoonful of salt.
Shake them about and then brown them
in the oven.

Cheese Straws

Ingredients

Grated Cheese
Flour
Butter
A pinch of salt &
    cayenne pepper
Ghee* to fry

Method

Take grated cheese and equal amounts of
flour and butter. Rub smooth with a little
salt and cayenne pepper. Roll out to a half
inch thick and fry in ghee.

Fritters

Ingredients

2 chittacks* of
    sujee*
4 eggs well beaten
4 chittacks*of milk
2 chittacks* of
    ghee*
Crushed sugar

Method

Mix the sujee* and eggs beating them well
together, gradually adding the milk. Melt
down 2 chittacks* of ghee* in a small
deep pan.

Pour into the boiling ghee,* in one spot,
a dessert spoonful of the mixture at a time.
Fry to a rich brown colour. Serve it up hot
sprinkled with crushed sugar.

Plantain Fritters

Ingredients

Method

12 ripe plantain
4 tbsp of fine sifted
  flour
½ cup of milk
Sugar to taste
Eggs

Prepare a batter of twelve ripe plantains*.
Mix the whole well together. Make into
cakes about a tablespoon.

Put them into melted ghee*. Fry them on
both sides till brown and serve hot.

Potato Cakes

Ingredients

Method

1 dessert spoon of
  baking powder
½ seer* potatoes
Little less than ¼
seer* flour

Boil the potatoes and mix the baking
powder and flour together and rub these
into the mashed potatoes. Roll out and
cut to normal bits and fry in ghee* till
it becomes a light brown colour. If it
becomes hard, a little milk may be added.

Potato Balls

Ingredients

Method

1 lb of potatoes
4 tbsp butter
2 tbsp cream
3 eggs
Bunch of parsley
Fine breadcrumbs
Hot fat to fry

Boil 1 pound of potatoes then while hot,
mash or rub them through a fine sieve.

Add 4 tablespoons of warm butter, 2
tablespoons of hot cream, the well beaten
yolks of 3 eggs, salt and pepper to taste.
2 teaspoons of chopped parsley and the
stiffly beaten whites of the eggs.

Chill and shape the mixture into balls with
floured hands. Brush over with beaten egg
and roll in fine bread crumbs and fry
in plenty of hot fat. Drain, garnish with
parsley and serve hot.

Singaras

Ingredients

1 seer* potatoes
1 cup panch-poran
1 cup oil
Puff pastry

Method

Pastry as per recipe p.126, but has to be kneaded, folded and left for some time. Would take about 2 hours. Better to get 1 lb puff pastry.

Peel and quarter a seer* of potatoes and put into an oven dish. Take a cupful of panch-parum* and roast under the grill till dark brown. Spread the roasted panch-parum* on a clean table and use a rolling pin to break the seed down.

Sprinkle the panch-poran* on to the potatoes and add a cupful of oil. Cover the dish and put into a moderate oven till the potatoes are cooked. Then mash the potatoes. Roll out the pastry on floured table. And cut the pastry into circles about the size of a small saucer.

Put a heaped tablespoon of the potato mixture into each of the pastry circles and make it into the form of a patty. Wet the edges and seal the patty. Insert about fifteen at a time into the middle of a moderate oven and let them bake till brown. Makes about 50.

(Editor's note: This is delicious but best eaten shortly after being made).

NOTES

BREAD

Soda Bread

Ingredients

¾ lb brown meal
¼ lb white flour
1 egg
Spoonful castor
    sugar
A pinch of salt &
    bicarbonate of
    soda
Butter milk

Method

Mix the brown meal and white flour
together. Rub with 1 egg and spoonful
of castor sugar. Same of bicarbonate of
soda and some salt. Rub all together into
the meal.

Take some thick sour milk or butter milk
and mix lightly into a light dough. Roll out
and make rounds flat (2 inch thick) loaf.
Tin floured and heated beforehand and put
in a very hot oven and bake for ¾ hour.
When half-done turn.

Same for white soda bread. Tea cakes may
be made in the same way with the addition
of sweet milk or butter. Baking powder is
needed in place of the soda and cut with
egg cup or wine glass.

Brown Bread

Ingredients

1 lb wholemeal
½ oz yeast
½ oz sugar
½ tsp salt
½ pint tepid cold
water

Method

Cream sugar and yeast, add the water.
Pour it into the middle of the sieved flour
and salt. Mix together and knead slightly.
Cover with a cloth and put to rise for ¾
hour. Knead the dough. Put it into
a floured tin. Leave for 20 minutes.
Bake in oven for 30 minutes.

Scoffa Loaf

Ingredients

1 ½ lbs flour or ¾ lbs
    atta*and ¾ lbs
    flour
1 ½ tsp salt
1 ½ tsp bicarbonate
    of soda
1 ½oz butter
¾ pint milk
    into which add
    2 tsp cream of
    tartar and 1 tbsp
    Golden Syrup

Method

Sift flour, salt and bicarbonate of soda into
a mixing bowl and rub in the butter until
like breadcrumbs.

Mix in the milk mixture and knead for 8 to
10 minutes. Turn onto a round cake plate
and cut across into 4 portions.

Bake for 40 to 45 minutes on a medium
hot oven. Cool on a wire tray.

Parathas

Ingredients

1lb brown or white
    flour
¼ lb Cookeen
Salt to luste

Method

Mix flour, salt and Cookeen together till it
becomes like bread crumbs. Add enough
slightly warm water to make a dough.

Divide into portions and roll out on
a floured board. Fry in hot Cookeen.

Chapatis

Ingredients

12 oz wholemeal
   flour
1 cup warm milk,
   buttermilk or
   water
1 tbsp oil
Salt to taste
Flour for dusting

Method

Mix the flour, salt and milk, buttermilk or water to form a dough. Put the dough on a surface that has been sprinkled with flour and knead in the oil for about ten minutes until smooth. Cover with damp cloth and allow to stand at room temperature for 20 minutes then make 12 balls out of the dough.

Coat each ball with flour and flatten to form a round. Then roll out to about 6 inches in diameter.

Heat a frying pan on high heat then reduce to moderate and place each chapatti to fry for about 30 seconds until the top begins to puff.

Turn over the chapatti and fry for another 30 seconds till the surface starts to puff. Remove and carry on frying the remaining chapatis the same way. Serve them hot.

Nut Buns

Ingredients

¼ seer* flour
1 ½ chittacks*
   butter
1 heaped tsp baking
   powder
1 ½ chittacks* sugar
1 ½ chittacks*
   grated nuts
2 tbsp milk
A pinch of salt

Method

Mix together the salt, flour and baking
powder. Rub in the butter. Add the sugar
and nuts and mix well.

Beat in the whipped egg and milk.
Bake in greased pans in moderate oven
for 15 minutes.

Buns

Ingredients

1lb of flour
6oz of butter
2tsp of baking
   powder
¼lb of sugar
¼ pint of milk

Method

Mix together quickly and bake immediately.
This will make 24 buns.

NOTES

_____

_____

_____

_____

_____

_____

_____

SALADS

Egg Lily Salad

Ingredients

Method

5 hard boiled eggs
Butter
Vinegar
Mustard
Salt & pepper
Mayonnaise
Spinach or lettuce
to serve

Drop hard boiled eggs into cold water
after taking them out of their shells.
Cut the white and remove the yolks.

Rub each yolk with 1 teaspoonful of butter.
1 of vinegar. 1 of mustard. Add salt and
pepper. Form into balls and put back into
whites. Serve on a mound of spinach or
lettuce with mayonnaise.

Indian Corn Salad

Ingredients

Method

Indian corn
Salt to taste
Mayonnaise
Dressing (See p.70)

Boil Indian corn with a little salt and
remove from the stalk. Put into dish with
thick mayonnaise dressing.

Tomato Cheese Salad

Ingredients

Method

4 good size ripe
  tomatoes
¼ lb pimento or
  Swiss cheese
  (diced)
French dressing
Lettuce

Scoop out centres of tomatoes and fill with
cheese and marinate with French dressing.
Serve very cold on crisp lettuce leaves with
cheese straws (p.19).

Pimento Cheese Salad

Ingredients

Method

¼ lb pimento
  cheese
5 tbsp cream
1 tsp gelatine
1 tbsp cold water
Green peppers
Lettuce
Salt
Pepper

Soften gelatine in cold water and dissolve
over hot water. Add this to the cheese
which has been grated and make a smooth
and moist cream.

Stuff peppers with the mixture and place
on ice. When very cold, slice in thin rings
and arrange rings on a bed of crispy
lettuce and serve with French dressing.

Bamboo Top Salad

Ingredients

1 large bamboo top
10 large prawns
Milk from 2
    coconuts
Salt
Onions
Green chillies
1 Lime

Method

Cut up the bamboo into the finest possible mince. Tie it up in a muslin and boil until quite tender. Put it aside to cool.

When cool, squeeze out the water till none remains. Turn out the bamboo.

Have the prawns boiled, shelled and minced fine. Mix the prawns with the bamboo, adding salt, finely chopped onions, green chillies, lime juice and the coconut milk. Mix all together.

Salad Dressing

Ingredients

2 chittacks* butter
1 tbsp flour
1 tsp salt, pepper
2 tbsp sugar
1 tsp mustard
½ cup vinegar
1 cup rich milk or
    cream
3 eggs (Unless
small then 4 eggs)

Method

Heat butter, add flour and stir but do not brown. Add milk and boil stirring all the time and boil up. Place pan in a saucepan of boiling water. Put back on the fire then add the vinegar.

Beat eggs and sugar together. Add salt, pepper, mustard and stir into the boiling mixture and let it cook a bit. Then take it off the fire and let it cool.

juice pepper & salt. Melt some
butter & fry the mixture in it until
the mixture be absorbed, then add
a little stock & remove from the
fire immediately the stock begins
to dry. Butter the shells & fill
the mixture. Take some finely
sifted bread crumbs, grind down
the coral & put it over the mixture
on the shells with the bread crumbs
& bits of butter & & bake for a few
minutes

Bamboo Curry.

Take the tops of a young bamboo cut it up very
fine make a rich prawn dopiaja curry add
the cut bamboo & cook well.

Bamboo top salad

1 large top, 10 large prawns, the milk from two

A well thumbed page from Grandmother's handwritten recipe book

NOTES

_____

_____

_____

_____

_____

_____

_____

SAVOURY
DISHES

Stuffed Mutton

Ingredients

3 lbs breast of
  mutton
1 carrot
1 onion
1 turnip
Bunch of herbs

For stuffing:
4oz breadcrumbs
Chopped suet
1oz of cooked ham
1 dessertspoonful of
  chopped parsley
¼tsp of powdered
  mixed herbs
½ lemon
Salt & pepper
1 egg
Milk, stock or water,
glaze

Method

Remove the skin and any fat from the
mutton and then bone it and put it skin-
side down on a board after wiping both
sides with a damp cloth.

Prepare the stuffing by mixing the
breadcrumbs, chopped suet, parsley,
chopped ham, herbs, and the grated rind
of half a lemon, salt and pepper in a
basin. Add a beaten egg, or enough milk
to moisten. Spread this over the mutton,
roll up and tie with a string. Put the bones,
sliced vegetables and the bunch of herbs at
the bottom of a pan.

Cover with stock or water and add a pinch
of salt. Place the mutton on top of this and
bring to the boil. Cover with greased paper
and the lid of the pan and simmer gently
either in the oven or on the top of the stove
for about 2 hours or until the mutton is
cooked, turning it over once.

When it is ready, remove the meat from
the pan, put it on a dish and cover it with
another dish and put a weight on it. Leave
until cold, then remove the string, trim the
ends and brush over with glaze. Garnish
with parsley, lettuce or watercress.

Chopped Steak in Potato Nests

Ingredients

½ lb potatoes
1 tbsp butter
2 tbsp cream
2 eggs
Onion juice
Salt & pepper to
   taste
Chopped steak
Green peas to serve

Method

To 3 cupfuls of hot mashed potatoes add 1 tablespoon of butter, 2 tablespoons of hot cream, the beaten yolks of 2 eggs, salt, pepper and onion juice to taste.

Beat until light and line a buttered baking dish, leaving a hollow in the centre.

Fill with hot chopped steak and reheat in the oven. Decorate with cooked green peas and serve.

Koftas

Ingredients

1lb lamb or beef
   mince
2 slices of white
   bread broken up
2 tbsp milk
1 cup chopped
   coriander
1 cup of chopped
   parsley
1 egg beaten
1 large onion
   grated
Optional chilli
Salt & pepper
1 tbsp
   Worcestershire
   Sauce
Oil for frying

Method

Put into a pan the bread, milk, coriander, parsley, Worcestershire sauce, onion, beaten egg and chilli, if required, and mix together.

Add the mince and mix well together. Make into balls. Spread breadcrumbs on a tray and roll each ball to cover them with the breadcrumbs. Fry in oil till well browned.

Yorkshire Puddings

Ingredients

1 egg
Salt
4oz flour
½ pint milk and
water

Method

Place flour in basin. Add egg in centre.
Add half the milk and water. Beat for
10 minutes. Add the rest of the milk
and water.

Let it stand for an hour or more. Bake in
a shallow tin of smoking fat.

Chicken Fried Rice

Ingredients

1 roast fowl (large)
¾ seer* prawns
½ lb bacon rashers
6 eggs
Salt to taste
Some ghee*
¾ seer* pillau rice
– fine grain

Method

First roast the fowl and shred the meat
into small pieces. Boil the prawns, fry the
bacon and set these aside.

In the bacon grease and some ghee*, fry
the rice till slightly brown. Now add water
to cover the rice 2 inches above and boil
the rice till done. Now add the minced
fowl, prawn and scrambled eggs, which
are done in the ghee* only, and the bacon
which should be minced too.

Mix together and salt to taste. Serve hot.
This serves eight people. In place of fowl,
mutton or beef could be used.

Spaghetti Milanese

Ingredients

4oz spaghetti
1oz margarine
Tomato sauce
1oz grated cheese
Little bit of pepper

Method

Cook the spaghetti in salted water for 15 minutes, then drain all the water. Melt the margarine in a pan, add to this the boiled spaghetti and toss this lightly. Add tomato sauce and heat but do not boil. Season to taste and pour into a dish while hot and top with the grated cheese. Serve at once.

Risotto

Ingredients

½ lb rice
1 pint stock
2 small onions
   chopped
3 oz grated cheese
2 oz margarine
4 tomatoes
2 oz raisins
Nutmeg
Salt & pepper

Method

Heat the margarine and fry the onions a light brown colour. Add the raisins and the rice and fry without browning. Add the stock, sliced tomatoes, nutmegs and seasoning. Put the lid on and cook gently for ½ hour or till rice is tender. Stir occasionally using a fork.

The risotto may be served with the grated cheese on top and browned a little in the oven.

Pepper Stuffed with Cheese

Ingredients

6 green peppers
1 tsp grated onion
¼ lb cheese grated
1 ½ cups
    breadcrumbs
2 tbsp butter
Salt & pepper

Method

Cut off thin slices from stem of peppers. Remove seeds and pith. Parboil peppers for 2 minutes, drain and fill with a mixture of the remaining ingredients.

Cover tops with cheese. Place on a greased baking dish and bake for 20 minutes in a moderate oven.

Sauteed Cauliflower with Cheese

Ingredients

2 cups cooked
    cauliflower
    broken into small
    pieces
2 tbps butter
2 tbps flour
¼ lb grated cheese
1 cup milk
Salt & pepper
Paprika

Method

Make a sauce of the butter, flour and milk. Add the seasonings. Add about ¾ of the cheese to the sauce and beat until smooth. Arrange alternate layers of cauliflower and sauce in a buttered baking dish.

Cover with buttered crumbs and add the remaining cheese. Bake in a hot oven until brown. If desired, cabbage may be used instead of cauliflower.

Cheddar Soufflé

Ingredients

Method

1 oz butter
½ oz flour
¼ pint milk
3 eggs (separated)
Salt and cayenne
    pepper
3 oz grated cheddar

Melt the butter. Remove pan from heat and add flour. Gradually add the milk stirring all the time. Return to heat and bring to the boil, stirring and continue cooking for 1 minute.

Allow to cool a little then add yolks, salt, cayenne pepper and grated cheese. Whisk egg whites until stiff. Stir in 1 spoonful of egg white, and then fold in the remainder with a tablespoon.

Pour into a buttered six inch dish and bake in the middle of a moderate hot oven (190°C) for 20 to 30 minutes. Serve immediately – 4 servings. (An extra egg white will make the soufflé rise even higher).

Cheese Potatoes

Ingredients

Method

4 large potatoes
2 eggs
1 oz butter
1 oz grated cheese
Salt & pepper

Roast the potatoes with skins on and cut a bit out of the sides of each one and take out nearly all the inside.

Mix 2 parts of this with the cheese, butter and eggs, well beaten, add seasoning. Put back into the potato skins and re-heat for 10 minutes.

Egg Cheese Toast

Ingredients

Method

3 eggs
1 ½ oz butter
2 oz grated cheese

Beat the eggs. Add the cheese and butter and mix. Stir over a gentle fire till thick. Serve on buttered toast.

Eggs au Gratin

Ingredients

Method

Eggs
White sauce
Butter
Cayenne pepper
Salt
Breadcrumbs

Lay slices of hard boiled eggs in the bottom of a pie dish, about half an inch thick. Over these put some good thick white sauce, made from corn flour or flour and milk, a little butter flavoured with grated cheese, cayenne pepper and a little salt. Put fine breadcrumbs over the top and put in the oven till brown.

Egg Novelty

Ingredients

4 eggs
Salt & pepper
White sauce
Grated cheese

Method

Hard boil 4 eggs and leave them in cold water for a minute or two to prevent the dark line that sometime comes between the yolk and white.

Grease a flat dish and slice the eggs into it. Sprinkle with salt and pepper. Pour over a cupful of white sauce into which 2 tablespoons of grated cheese have been stirred. A little more grated cheese can be put on later.

Egg Chow

Ingredients

Eggs
Onions
Dry chillies
Jeera*
Garlic
Saffron
Salt
Ghee*

Method

Chop 6 large onions finely for 3 or 4 eggs. Grind 6 or less large dry chillies, a little jeera*, 4 pieces of garlic, a small bit of saffron and a little salt.

Fry the onions in ghee* till brown, throw in the raw eggs and put on a slow fire and keep on stirring all the time.

Fry the curry stuff (ground chillies etc). When nice and brown pour all together. Water only a little to prevent the eggs sticking to the chattie*.

Egg Omlette

Ingredients	Method
Eggs Parsley Chillies Tomatoes Mint Onions	Beat egg yolks and whites separately. (Whites to be beaten to a thick froth). Beat thoroughly the yolks with parsley, chillies, tomatoes, mint and onions. Add salt to taste. Then mix with whites and fry.

Karti Kebab*(1)

Ingredients	Method
2 lbs beef, mutton or veal 2 tbsp mustard oil 4 tbsp ground onions 1 tsp ground chillies ½ tsp ground ginger ¼ a teaspoon ground garlic 1 tsp ground turmeric 1 tsp of salt 1 cup of thick tyre* ½ teaspoon of coriander seed The juice of 1 large lemon and a little ghee*	Take 2 pounds of beef, mutton or veal. Remove the bones and chop the meat without mincing or cutting through. Mix well together all the ground condiments including oil and tyre. Into which steep the meat, turning it over occasionally to all the mixture. After a while cut up the meat into squares of equal size and continue to keep them in the mixture for fully an hour. Press the squares of meat on a silver metal skewer and roast over a slow charcoal fire, blasting the whole tome with ghee* until a rich brown colour.

Karti Kebab* (2)

Ingredients

Method

1 large onion
1 tsp ginger
1 tsp garlic
½ tsp chilli
½ tsp coriander
½ tsp turmeric
¼ tsp mustard
  powder
1 tbsp lemon juice
1 lb pork, beef or
  lamb
¾ lb junket

Chop onion in small pieces. Chop up the
meat and mix with all the ingredients and
allow to marinate overnight. Place in a
saucepan and add 2 tablespoons of oil.

Boil on a slow heat until it is dry, stirring
all the time to stop the meat sticking to the
pan. A gravy should form around the meat
which should take an hour and a half.
Add salt to taste.

Nice in parathas with lemon juice and
sliced onions.

Pork Karti Kebab (3)

Ingredients

Method

1 ½ lbs pork fillet
5 dessert spoons
Patak madras curry
Paste
3 dessert spoons
Yogurt

Mix the curry paste with the yogurt. Chop
the pork into small 1 inch square cubes
and put into the mix and stir well. Allow
to marinate overnight. Put into the oven
at 180°C for about 1 hour or more if
necessary. You can also use lamb or beef
if wanted.

*(Editor's note: My wife makes this recipe with ingredients
obtained from local supermarkets or Asian shops. It is quite
easy to make and is delicious served with parathas, chapatis, or
lentils and rice. Needs a side dish of sliced onions and lemon to
complete the treat).*

Bouboutie

Ingredients

1 thick slice
  white bread
250 ml milk
1 large onion
  finely chopped
25ml cooking oil
2 eggs
37.5ml lemon juice
10ml curry powder
5ml sugar
5ml salt
Pinch of pepper
500mg minced
Mutton or beef
12.5ml fruit chutney

Method

Soak the bread in the milk. Using a large frying pan sauté the onion in the cooking oil until it is lightly browned. Combine the lemon juice, curry powder, salt, sugar and pepper and stir mixture into the onion.

Squeeze most of the milk out of the bread, keeping the milk for later. Mash the bread and add it to the onion mixture. Add the minced meat, 1 egg and 150ml of milk and mix well. Add the chutney and allow the mixture to cook for a while, stirring often.

Pre heat the oven to 180°C. Grease an oven proof dish. Transfer the meat mixture to the dish. Place in the oven for a few minutes. Beat the remaining egg and the remaining milk. Pour the mixture over the Boboutie. Bake for 30 minutes and serve hot.

Wirral Eggs

Ingredients

Eggs
1 oz breadcrumbs
1 tsp mustard
Chopped parsley
Grated cheese

Method

Soak 1 ounce of breadcrumbs in a stock of gravy. Beat up 1 or more eggs and add the breadcrumbs and also a teaspoon of mustard, a teaspoon of chopped parsley, a teaspoon of grated cheese. Spread the mixture on bits of warm toast. Sprinkle grated cheese over and brown in the oven.

Crabs in Shell

Ingredients

Whole crabs
Onions
Ginger juice
Salt & pepper
Butter
Breadcrumbs
Lemon juice

Method

Clean and boil the crabs. Remove them out of the shell. Pick and clean them well and reserve the shell for dressing.

Chop and mince the crab. Add some onions and ginger juice, a little lemon juice, pepper and salt.

Melt some butter and fry the mixture in it until the mixture is absorbed, then add a little stock and remove from the fire, immediately the stock begins to dry.

Butter the shells and fill the mixture. Take some finely sifted breadcrumbs, grind down the coral* and put it over the mixture on the shells with the breadcrumbs and bits of butter and bake for a few minutes.

NOTES

_____

_____

_____

_____

_____

_____

_____

CURRIES

Curry Powder

Ingredients

Method

6 tbsp ground
onions
4½ tbsp fresh
yellow
ground turmeric
3 tbsp ground garlic
3 tbsp ground
ginger
2 tbsp each ground
coriander and
cumin
1 tbsp of ground
dry red chillies
1 tbsp salt
½ seer* ghee*
or butter

All ingredients to be ground using as little
water as possible in the grinding. Melt the
butter in a saucepan and when boiling add
the ground onions and garlic and cook for
ten minutes but do not let them brown.

Add all the other ingredients and cook
till the ingredients brown and stick to the
bottom and sides of the pan and no water
is left. Stir constantly to prevent burning.

Bottle when cool and before sealing, pour
over the top a little clarified butter or
ghee* which has been brought to the boil
and allowed to cool but not cold.

Curry Paste

Ingredients

Method

1 large onion
2 cloves of garlic
2 tsp turmeric
3 large tbsp corn
oil
2 large tbsp curry
powder (See
above)
1 large tbsp garam
masala*
Water

Slice onions and garlic and fry in the oil
till golden brown. Mix turmeric, curry
powder and garam masala* in about a cup
of water. Add this to the fried onions and
fry for a little while. Put all the ingredients
into the oven and cook till quite brown.

You can add meat and salt to taste to
make a good curry. When meat is tender,
it is ready to serve with rice.

Curry

*Chicken; beef; lamb; egg (hard boiled first); cauliflower; peas;
potato mixed together*

Ingredients

Method

1 lb any of the
  above
1 large onion
2 cloves of garlic
2 tsp turmeric
3 large tbsp of
  corn oil
2 large tbsp curry
  powder (see left)
1 large tbsp garam
masala*

Slice the onions and the garlic and fry
them in the oil till golden brown.

Mix the turmeric, curry powder and garam
masala* in a cupful of water. Add this to
the fried onions and garlic and fry for a
little while.

Put the ingredients into the oven and
cook till quite brown. Add the meat or
vegetables and salt to taste. When tender
ready to serve with rice.

Kofte* Curry

Method

Make Koftas as per Kofta recipe (p.37) then use above
curry recipe.

Vegetable or Meat Curry

Ingredients

1 lb meat or
  vegetables
Curry powder
Onion
Butter
3 tbsp hot water

Method

Using the curry powder on p.50 –
1 tablespoon of the mixture for 1lb
meat or vegetables.

Melt a little butter or dripping in a
saucepan and fry a small onion finely
chopped. Remove the onion and set
aside. Now in the grease add the curry
powder mixed into a liquid paste with 3
tablespoons hot water and cook stirring
constantly till it begins to stick in the pan.

Now add the meat or the vegetables, stir
well and brown in the curry powder for ten
minutes then add 2 breakfast cups of hot
water and allow to simmer till the meat
or vegetables are tender and all the paste
absorbed. Serve with the fried onions.

Kurella (Karela) Curry

Ingredients

Kurella
Salt
Onions
Vegetables
Sugar & salt to taste

Method

Scrape the green skins of the Kurella till
almost smooth. Cut up as usual, removing
seeds. Add sufficient salt. Boil for about
30 minutes then drain off the water.

Cut up 4 good sized onions. Fry usual
curry ingredients in oil thoroughly, then
add the vegetables and cut up onions.
Cook for about 20 minutes adding sugar
and salt to taste.

Jhal Frazee*

Ingredients

Mutton or beef
Onions
Chillies
1 tsp salt
Ghee*

Method

Cut up into small squares of less than an inch of either cold mutton or beef, rejecting bones. Add a large quantity of onions sliced, some chillies and a teaspoon of salt.

Warm a chittack* of ghee*. Throw into it the meat, onions and chillies. Allow to simmer or fry, stirring the whole time till the onions are quite tender.

Chicken Curry

Ingredients

Dhunnia*
1 chittack* or 2 oz
   of ghee*
2 breakfast cups of
   water
1 tsp of salt
4 tsp of ground
   onions
1 tsp each of
   ground turmeric
   & chillies
½ tsp of ground
   ginger
¼ tsp of garlic

Method

To suit the taste of those who may like it, half teaspoon of coriander or dhunnia* may be added, which should be roasted before being ground.

Observe the directions for cooking. Take the usual half size chicken and divide it from each joint. Warm the pot. Melt in it the ghee* and immediately it begins to bubble, throw in it all the ingredients, stirring it until quite brown, then put in the cut up chicken and salt and cook until a light brown colour.

Add the water and allow it to simmer over a slow fire until the chicken is quite tender and the gravy reduced to about half its original quantity. Time for cooking will take from half to three quarters of an hour. Kid (lamb) or duck curry are made in the same way as above.

Bhoona Kitcheree

Ingredients

Rice
Dhal*
12 large onions
2 chittack* or 4
  ounces of ghee*
Ginger
Salt & pepper
Cloves
Bay leaves
Cinnamon sticks

Method

Take the weight of dhal* in rice (good rice). Take 12 large onions and cut them up lengthwise into fine slices. Warm up 2 chts* or 4ozs of ghee* but before doing so, take good care to warm the pot and while bubbling, throw in the onions removing them as soon as they are light brown colour.

Set the onions aside and throw them in the dhal* and rice, having previously allowed all the water in which they were washed to drain off. Fry until the dhal* and rice have absorbed all the ghee*, then add a few slices of ginger, some pepper and salt to taste, a few cloves, a few bay leaves and a stick or two of cinnamon.

Mix well together; add as much water as will cover the rice & dal* and put on the cover to let it cook on a very slow fire, reducing the same from time to time as the water gets absorbed.

Care must be taken not to let the kitcheree burn, which must be prevented by occasionally shaking the pot or stirring its contents with a wooden spoon. Serve it quite hot.

Bhoona kitcheree of green peas or gram dhal* - the chunna* or gram dhal* makes a very nice kitcheree but as it is rather hard, it should be soaked in cold water an hour or so before frying it with the rice.

Chicken Pillau

Ingredients

Whole chicken
1 lb beef or mutton
2 breakfast cups of
   water
12 onions
4 chittack* or 4 oz
   of ghee*
1 seer* rice
Cloves
Cardamoms
Cinnamon sticks
Peppers
Salt & pepper

Method

Take a good sized chicken, clean and boil
it with 1 pound of beef or mutton in 2 cups
of water. Season it with onions, ginger
and salt. When sufficiently cooked, but yet
quite firm, remove the chicken and set it
and the gravy aside.

Cut up twelve onions lengthways into fine
slices. Warm your pot, then melt 2 chts*
or 4 ounces of ghee* and as it bubbles,
throw in the sliced onions and fry to a
light brown, then remove the onions and
put aside.

The put in 1 seer* of fine rice which has
been washed and drained well and fry.
Throw in a few cloves, 4 or 5 cardamoms,
a few sticks of cinnamons, some peppers
and 1 tablespoon of salt.

Mix up the whole and pour over it the
gravy in which the chicken and meat were
boiled, or as much of it as will entirely
cover the rice.

Close the pot with a close fitting cover
set on a slow fire. As the gravy continues
to decrease, reduce the fire. Brown the
chicken in a pot of ghee* and serve.

Chicken Country Captain

Ingredients

Whole chicken
Ghee*
Onions
Turmeric
Chillies
Salt

Method

Cut up in the usual way an ordinary chicken. Warm the ghee* and fry the sliced onions and when brown set aside, fry the ground turmeric and chillies, then throw in the chicken and salt and continue to fry, stirring the whole till the chicken is tender. Serve it over the fried onions.

Bindaloo (Vindaloo 1)

Ingredients

1 seer* good fat
   meat
2 chittacks* ginger
1 chittack * garlic
½ oz of chillies
1 large turmeric
Vinegar
Mustard oil
Jeera*
Pepper

Method

Have the ingredients ground rather coarse. Add vinegar to the ground ingredients. Add the meat, soak for a few hours. Burn the mustard oil properly. Allow to cool for a few minutes then add to the rest and cook till ready.

Before served sprinkle with roasted jeera* and pepper fried and pounded.

Vindaloo (2)

Ingredients

Method

1 lb beef
1 garlic
1 tsp ground ginger
1 tsp turmeric
2 tsp jeera
¼ cup vinegar
½ cup oil
½ tsp sugar
Salt to taste

Mix all the ingredients in a bowl (not saucepan or metal). Add vinegar, oil and meat and allow to soak overnight or, at least, a minimum of 2 hours before cooking. Cook till meat is tender then sprinkle with dhannia* and jeera* before serving.

(Editor's note: What! No Chillies?)

Fish Mooloo

Ingredients

Method

White fish
Coconut
3 or 4 chillies
Onions
Half a garlic
Ghee*
Vinegar
Ginger
Salt
Whole pepper

Fry the fish and let it cool. Scrape a coconut and put a tea cup of hot water into it.

Rub it well, strain it and put aside, then put 2 spoonfuls more of water, strain this also; cut up 3 or 4 green chillies and as many onions as you like with half a garlic.

Fry them with a little ghee* and whilst frying put the last straining of the coconut water with the ingredients till it is dry; then add the first water of the nut and pour the whole over the fish, with some vinegar, ginger, whole pepper and salt.

Mutton or Lamb Korma

Ingredients

1 lb mutton or lamb
1 dsp finely bruised green ginger
1 heaped tsp parched, ground and sifted coriander seed
1 tsp finely ground black pepper
1 tsp finely ground turmeric
½ tsp of each of finely ground cardamoms
Cinnamon and cloves
1 tsp salt
1 tsp flour
¼ lb clarified butter or ghee*
1 large white onion
4 or 5 cloves of garlic finely sliced
4 dozen well ground sweet almonds
1 small cup of sour milk or cream
Juice of lemon

Method

Make a pint of clear stock from the bones and scraps of meat prior to starting the korma. Mix the pieces of meat in a bowl with the ginger and leave for a few minutes.

Melt the ghee* or clarified butter in a pan and fry the onions and garlic till they begin to brown. Gradually stir in the flour, ground spices and salt and keep stirring for 5 minutes, diluting the mixture with a little of the stock to prevent burning.

Put in the meat and continue to stir for another 5 minutes then pour in the remainder of the stock and allow to simmer till the meat is tender, then add an infusion of the ground almonds and a teacupful of hot water squeezed through a muslin and lastly a little sour milk or cream, with a little sugar and allow to simmer for a further ten minutes. The juice of a lemon may be added. The Korma Curry must be cooked on a slow fire and allowed to simmer.

Quorema (Korma) Curry (2)

Ingredients

2 lb mutton
2 ½ chittacks* ghee*
1 tsp ground chillies
1 cup tyre*
1 tsp salt
4 tsp ground onions
1 tsp coriander seed
6 small sticks
  ground
  cinnamon
½ tsp ground ginger
¼ tsp ground garlic
6 or 10 peppercorns
4 or 5 ground
  cloves
5 or 6 ground
  cardamoms
2 or 3 bay leaves
¼ cup water
12 large onions cut
  lengthwise
Juice of 1 lemon
2 lbs mutton

Method

Take 2 pounds of good fat mutton
and cut it into pieces. Warm the ghee*
and fry in it the sliced onions and set
aside when brown. Then fry all the ground
ingredients and spices. When quite brown,
throw in the mutton and allow the whole
to brown, after which add the tyre* and
hot spices, peppers, bay leaves water
and fried onions.

Close the lid on the pan and let it simmer
over a slow for an hour and a half to
2 hours.

Dhal* (Lentils)

Ingredients

Method

2 breakfast cups of
  red lentils
1 tsp turmeric
1 onion
Butter
1 tsp garam masala

Take 2 cups of red lentils. Wash well and strain out the water. Put into a dish. Add a teaspoon of turmeric and salt to taste. Cover the lentils with about 2 inches of water above and put a lid on the dish. Put into oven, about mid heat, till water is absorbed then take out of the oven.

Chop a large onion and fry in a pan of butter till brown. Put a teaspoon of garam masala into the onions, then strain the lentils into the pan and mix well.

Dhal* (Lentil) Soup and Sippits

Ingredients

Method

(See above recipe)
Toasted bread

All you have to do is to water down the lentils (above) and mix well. This soup goes well with sippits (croutons). Sippits are made from a slice of toasted bread cut into squares a third of an inch thick and fry then till crisp.

Chicken Malay Doopiaja

Ingredients

Chicken pieces
1 ½ chittacks*
   ghee*
1 ½ tsp salt
4 tsp ground onions
1 tsp ground
   turmeric
1 tsp ground chillies
½ tsp ground ginger
¼ tsp ground garlic
1 cup strong
   coconut milk
12 onions cut
lengthways into fine
slices

Method

Cut up the chicken in the usual manner.
Warm the ghee*. Fry and set aside the
onions, then fry the ground condiments
after which add the chicken and salt.

When fried brown, pour in the coconut
milk and the fried onions, finely chopped,
and allow to simmer over a slow fire. The
Malay Doopiaja will be ready in an hour.

Bamboo Curry

Ingredients

(See above recipe)
Young bamboo

Method

Take the top of a young bamboo. Cut it up
very fine. Make a nice Doopiaja Curry (As
above). Add the cut bamboo and cook well.

Aloo Dum (1)

Ingredients

1 lb potatoes
4 oz ghee*
2 oz dhal*
1 oz condiment
    paste
2 drams hot spice
    powder
Bay leaves
Sugar & salt to taste

Method

The paste is obtained by brazing the following with water. Turmeric, chillies, coriander seed, black pepper and ginger.

The seasoning powder is obtained by powdering the following spices viz. cinnamon, cloves and small cardamoms.

Boil new potatoes in plenty of water and drain when soft and tender. Peel them while hot and smear them with dhal* and condiment paste.

Melt the ghee* on an iron pan and throw in some bay leaves. When they are singed put in the potatoes and enough water for stewing. Add a pinch of sugar and salt to taste. Allow to simmer for a few minutes and remove when dry. Dredge with hot spice powder and serve.

Aloo Dum (2)

Ingredients

2 dessert spoons
    panch-param*
3 large spoons oil
1 large or 2 small
    cloves garlic
A few peppercorns
    and cloves
1 tsp turmeric
1 lb potatoes

Method

Roast panch pooram*, peppercorns and cloves under the toaster and crush till very fine. Fry garlic in oil with turmeric and add the crushed spices to this, then the potatoes and salt.

Put in the oven and cook till potatoes are tender. (Keep the pan covered).

Gram Dhal* Curry

Ingredients

Split peas
Curry paste (p.50)
Meat or hard boiled
eggs

Method

To make gram dhal* curry, just soak split peas (amount of your choice and taste) overnight. Then put them into the curry paste (p.50) and add meat or hard boiled eggs.

Mattar* Paneer*

Peas and Indian cheese in spicy sauce

Ingredients

8 oz Paneer*
Oil for frying
2 peeled medium
  onions
8 oz peas
1 inch piece of
  fresh peeled
  ginger
1 green chilli
3 medium tomatoes
1 pint milk
Salt to taste
A few fresh chopped
  coriander leaves
1 tsp each cumin
  seeds and
  turmeric powder
1 tsp each ground
  coriander and
  garam masala
2 tsp paprika
½ oz chilli powder

Method

Cut the prepared paneer* in ½ inch cubes.
Heat the oil 180c/350f. Put a few paneer
pieces in at a time and fry until golden
from all sides. Drain and leave aside.
Finely chop onions, ginger and green chilli
and make smooth into a paste.

Heat 3 tablespoons of oil in the saucepan
and fry the cumin seeds for 1 minute. Add
onions, ginger and green chilli paste. Stir
fry for 10 – 12 minutes until lightly brown.

Add turmeric, coriander, paprika and
chopped tomatoes. Stir continuously until
tomatoes are reduced to a pulp.

Add peas, salt and chilli powder. Reduce
the heat. Cover the saucepan and steam
cook for 5 minutes.

Pour water into the sauce pan and bring to
the boil over a high flame then simmer for
20 minutes on a low heat.

Put in the fried paneer and cook until
paneer* has absorbed some sauce and
peas are tender.

Stir in garam* masala*. Before serving,
sprinkle with chopped coriander. Serve
with rice or poories with any meat or
vegetable dish. Serves 4. Preparation time
6 hours. Cooking time 45 minutes.

Boiled Rice (fluffy)

Ingredients

Method

2 breakfast cups
of basmati rice

2 cups of basmati rice washed well to
remove as much starch as possible. Put
into a saucepan and fill with water.
Bring it to the boil and let it simmer.
Keep checking till rice is cooked.
Then strain well.

(Editor's note: I was brought up on dhal
baht (lentils and rice). Lentils are good to
add to a curry and rice. Try it).

Pillau Rice

Ingredients

Method

1½ seers*of rice
4 chittacks* ghee

Fry the rice for half an hour or more in
the ghee* and then put it in the soup. Let
it boil on a slow fire until the rice is quite
melted. If need be a little more soup may
be added. Enough for 10 people.

Yellow Rice

Ingredients

Method

1 large cup rice
1 tsp turmeric
1 large cup
   desiccated
   coconut
   (fine cut)
Oil to fry the rice
Coconut milk

Soak the coconut in boiling water for a
couple of hours. Fry the rice very lightly.
Squeeze the milk from the coconut and add
turmeric and a little salt.

Mix this and add to the fried rice and cook
on a very low fire till rice is tender and
ready for serving. This must be kept warm
for serving.

Dhal* Poories

Ingredients

1 lb gram dhal*
1 lb ghee*
2 lb flour
2 oz mustard oil
Spices and peppers

Method

Boil the gram dhal+*for half hour. Sieve the mass into the mustard oil. Remove when doughy. Divide the mass into small pieces about the size of a marble.

Then knead the flour working in an ounce or two of ghee* to make the process tender and crisp. Make some small balls out of it. Put in 1 of the marble balls prepared above and close up. This needs a little manipulation and the quantity of the small balls to be adjusted so that it does not bulge out when pressure is applied in subsequent operations.

Roll out the loaded balls into flat circular cakes on an oiled surface, with an oiled roller. Take a teaspoon of ghee* on a pan slightly curved at the centre and after smearing both sides of the cakes with ghee*, fry in the pan.

Junket* and Mint Sauce

Ingredients

4 oz plain junket*
½ tsp chillies
½ tsp salt
1 tsp garam masala
2 tsp mint sauce
concentrated

Method

Blend all the ingredients in a small bowl. Serve with Shish Kebab, Allo Laras, Pakoras, Onion Bhaji and Singaras.

The chunna or gran dall makes a very nice kitcheeree, but as it is rather hard it should be soaked in cold water an hour or so before frying it with the rice.

Chicken Pillow.

Take a good size chicken, clean & boil it with one pound of beef or mutton, in two cups of water, season it with onions ginger & salt. When sufficiently cooked, but yet quite firm remove the chicken & set it & the gravy aside. Cut up twelve onions lenght ways into fine slices. Warm your pot, then melt two chits oz or four oz of ghee & as it bubbles throw in the sliced onions, & fry to a light brown, then remove the onions & put aside. Then put in 1 seer of fine rice which have washed well & drained well & fry, throw in a few cloves four or five cardamons a few sticks of cinmanons some pepper & one dessert spoon of salt. Mix up the whole & pour over it the gravy

Mother's recipe for Chicken Pillau which can be found on page 55

67

NOTES

SAUCES, PICKLES & PRESERVES

Mayonnaise Sauce (1)

Ingredients

Egg yolk
½ tsp French
   mustard
¼ tsp salt
Pepper
½ pint best salad
   oil
Tarragon vinegar
½ tsp cream

Method

Put the yolk of an egg into a basin, add ½ teaspoon of French mustard, ¼ of teaspoonful of salt and a pinch of pepper. Stir quickly with a wooden spoon and add ½ pint of best salad oil, first drop by drop then more quickly and at intervals a few drops of tarragon vinegar. By stirring well this mixture should have the consistency of very thick cream.

Lastly add ½ a teaspoonful of cream, stirring all the while. A little cold water may be added if the sauce is too thick. In hot weather the mayonnaise should be put into a basin of crushed ice.

Mayonnaise Dressing (2)

Ingredients

2 tbsp mustard
2 tbsp sugar
1 teaspoon salt
1 egg
1 tsp cornflour
8 tbsp milk
2 tbsp butter
6 tbsp vinegar

Method

Mix mustard, sugar, salt and cornflour together. Break in the egg and beat well. Put the milk on the stove and add the mixture. Cook as a thin custard and when almost done, add the vinegar. Let it bubble once or twice and remove. Stir all the time when cooking. This will keep for ages and is very nice for sandwiches with slices of cucumber.

(Editor's note: This is very good. I have enjoyed it over the years).

Home-made Worcestershire Sauce (1)

Ingredients

Method

¼ chillies
2 oz raisins
1 oz salt
1 lb sugar
¼ oz pepper
½ oz garlic
12 cloves
1 quart vinegar

All the ingredients, except the sugar,
to be ground in the vinegar. Strain through
some muslin.

Burn half the quantity of sugar to a dark
brown to give it a proper colour. Add the
vinegar with the ingredients and the rest of
the sugar and boil for about 10 minutes.
The longer it keeps, the more it improves.

Home-made Worcestershire Sauce (2)

Ingredients

Method

2 quarts vinegar
4 drams powdered
    pimento
2 drams powdered
    cloves
2 drams powdered
black pepper
4 oz powdered
    mustard
2 drams powdered
    Jamaican ginger
4 ozs salt
4 oz shallots
8 oz tamarind
2 pints sherry
2 oz curry powder
2 drams capsicum

Mix well all together. Simmer for an hour
or so. Strain it and then remove the course
particles. Then bottle it.

Caper Sauce

Ingredients

1 oz of butter
1 oz of flour
3 gills* milk
1 tbsp of capers
Vinegar
Salt and pepper

Method

Melt the butter and draw to one side.
Mix well, add milk and boil it up and
add the capers.

Tomato Sauce

Ingredients

3 seers* tomatoes
2 bottles vinegar
1 chittack* salt
4 chittacks* sugar
    or more to taste
Mustard seeds
1 tollah
1 chittack* ginger
½ chittack* garlic
    peeled
½ chittack* chillies

Method

Warm the tomatoes over a slow fire and
strain through a net. Grind the rest of the
ingredients in vinegar.

Mix the strained tomatoes and ingredients
together and cook till it is reduced to half
the quantity. Keep stirring, cool and bottle.

Bringal* Kussundi*

Ingredients

2 seers bringal*
2 chittacks* ginger
2 chittacks* garlic
½ chittack* chillies
3 pieces turmeric
Salt
1 dessert spoon
   dhunnia*
1 tsp mixed seeds
½ tsp jeera*
Vinegar
Bottle of mustard oil
1 breakfast cup of
sugar

Method

The bringal* to be cut up into squares. All the ingredients to be ground in vinegar.

The oil to be burnt and the ingredients to be browned in it, then add the sugar and salt and put in the bringal*. No water to be put in.

Cashmere Chutney

Ingredients

100 mangoes
Half seer* garlic
Half seer* ginger
1 chittack* dried
   chillies
¼ seer* raisins
¼ seer* almonds
   peeled
1 seer* sugar
2 bottles vinegar

Method

Fifty mangoes to be sliced and salted for 1 day and put in the sun the next day. The other fifty to put into vinegar with ground garlic, ginger and chillies.

The whole to be put in the sun with 2 bottles of vinegar for 2 days. Then make a syrup of the vinegar and sugar.

Mix the whole together, adding the sliced almonds and raisins after which expose to the sun for 15 days and if after this you see that the chutney is rather dry, add some more vinegar.

(Editor's note: Another 100 mangoes and 15 day sun in the UK!!).

Acid Plum Sweet Chutney

Ingredients

½ seer* plums
    smashed
¼ seer* jagry*
1 chittack* ginger
½ chittack* garlic
½ chittack* chillies
1 tablespoon of salt
½ bottle vinegar

Method

All to be boiled together.

Apple Chutney

Ingredients

2 Golden Delicious
    apples, cored and
    sliced
1 tomato - chopped
1 inch fresh ginger
    peeled and
    chopped
1 medium onion
    peeled and sliced
1 green chilli
1 tsp salt
2 tbsp lemon juice
2 tsp sugar
1 tsp garam masala
½ tsp chilli powder
Small bunch of
coriander leaves
washed and
coarsely chopped

Method

Place all the ingredients together. Add a little water and blend the mixture to a smooth paste.

Kussundi* Chutney

Ingredients

60 green mangoes
2 chittacks* white
    mustard seed
    without husk
6 chittacks* ginger
    peeled
3 chittacks* salt
4 chittacks* garlic
    peeled
4 chittacks* chillies
1 ½ seers*
    tamarind without
    seeds
1 chittack* turmeric
2 ½ seer* mustard
oil

Method

Peel the mangoes, salt them and dry the
next day in the sun. Slice half of them and
pound half. Grind the other ingredients
very fine with vinegar and mix all together.
Sun in a jar, well closed, for 15 days.

Kurella* (Karela) Pickle

Ingredients

20 good sized
    kurellas*
2 chittacks* garlic
2 chittacks* ginger
2 chittacks* jeera*
2 chittacks* mustard
    seed
2 ½ chittacks* dried
    chillies
1 bottle malt
    vinegar
1 bottle mustard oil

Method

Wash and wipe the kurellas, then cut into
long strips. Remove the seeds and salt
them and allow them to soak in a good
sized dish for 24 hours. The shake well in
the salt water, remove and place on a flat
dish to dry in the sun for a day.

Clean and grind all the ingredients
separately in vinegar. (No water used).
Bring the oil to boiling point and fry all
the ingredients till cooked.

Add the kurellas and the balance
vinegar and a little salt and sugar to
taste. Boil for about 30 minutes and
bottle when cold.

Tomato Pickle

This is a delicious pickle and much appreciated by everyone.

Ingredients

Method

8 lb of ripe
  tomatoes
1 bottle of mustard
  oil
1 lb sugar
2 oz salt
6 oz each of green
  ginger and
  minced
  garlic
1 oz methe*
3 oz jeera*
1 bottle vinegar
4 oz each of
mustard seed and
red chillies

Clean and roast the methe, jeera and
mustard seed and grind them in vinegar
with the chillies.

Heat the oil and fry the methe, jeera and
mustard seeds in it, till the raw smell
disappears. Gradually put in the tomatoes
and half a bottle of vinegar. Then add the
sugar, salt, ginger and garlic.

Simmer on a slow fire with the pan
uncovered until the oil floats on the top,
stirring occasionally to prevent burning.

Green Tomato Pickle

Ingredients

Method

2 lbs green
  tomatoes
½ lb onions
1 lb cucumber
Salt
Malt vinegar
½ ounces mixed
  spices
1 oz chillies or
  cayenne

Slice tomatoes, onions and cucumbers.
Lay them in a bottle in layers, with salt
between them and leave for a night. Put in
a pressure pan. Cover with vinegar.
Add spices and chillies.

Calves Feet Jelly

Ingredients	Method
6 Trotters	The trotters to be boiled until the soup is quite thick, then allowed to cool and drain through a duster.
4 Limes	
4 eggs	
2 cups sugar	
1 wine glass brandy	Beat up the eggs and add the sugar and mix until the sugar is melted, then add the soup. Stir well and add the lime juice. The mixture is to be poured from one saucepan to another from a good height about six times, then put in the cinnamon. Now boil on a slow fire and when it cracks pour in the brandy. Strain through a double jharan* and stand in a cool place to set.
1 piece of cinnamon	

Sweet Sliced Mango

Ingredients	Method
5 seers* mangoes	First boil the mangoes with a bottle and half of vinegar very slightly, then pour into a dish to cool.
2 ½ bottles vinegar	
4 seers* sugar	
1 seer* raisins	
½ seer* ginger chopped fine	Take the other bottle of vinegar and mix it with the sugar and cook it to a thin syrup. Put in the raisins, salt, ginger, garlic, chillies and almonds. Last of all, put in the mangoes and cook till done.
1 chittack* garlic chopped fine	
2 chittacks* salt	
1 seer* almonds sliced	
2 chittacks* chillies chopped fine	

Mango Kussundi*

Ingredients

100 mangoes
1 bottle vinegar
4 chittacks* ginger
2 chittacks* garlic
2 chittacks* chillies
2 chittacks* mustard
  seeds (if liked)
2 seers* oil
  (or more)
Ground turmeric

Method

Cut the mangoes in half and take out the stones. Pick each with a fork and salt (1 cup full). Allow the mangoes to stand for a day. Put half the seeds in the oil with 2 pieces of ground turmeric and allow it to burn well.

Mix all the other ingredients, which must be ground in vinegar. Stuff the mangoes and tie with a thread. Fill into wide mouth bottles.

Cover with the oil and sun, till done. About 1 month.

(Editor's note. Not sure about the 100 mangoes or about the sun in the UK...)

Balichow

Ingredients

2 lbs tomatoes
2 lbs tamarind
4 chittacks* prawns
4 chittacks* garlic
4 chittacks* ginger
1 bottle mustard oil
1 bottle vinegar
1 onion
Salt to taste (about
1 chittack*)

Method

Put the tomatoes and tamarind together and boil in water adding a quarter of a bottle of vinegar till the water begins to dry off. Grind the onion, garlic and ginger each by itself using a little vinegar when grinding.

Put the mustard oil in a pan and cook with a clove or two of garlic till the garlic turns brown, taking care not to let it catch fire. Then lift it off the fire and add the crushed onion. Replace it on the fire and cook till the onion turns brown. Add the crushed garlic and ginger and continue cooking.

The tomatoes and tamarind should be strained though a course cloth and the balichow added bit by bit as the straining is being done. Mix well, then add the rest of the vinegar when straining which will help to mix things well and cook for a bit longer. Balichow can be kept in well-sealed bottles for use at later dates.

To Preserve Lime Juice

Ingredients

Method

3 cups lime juice
2 cups sugar
¼ cup boiling water
4 grams potassium
metabisulfite

Squeeze out the lime juice and put it in a
bowl with the sugar until it dissolves and
add the water. Lastly stir in the potassium
melabisulfite mixing thoroughly.

Put in bottles and cork tightly. Will keep
for months or even years.

Gooseberry Jam

Ingredients

Method

Gooseberries
Sugar
Cinnamon stick

1 seer* of gooseberries. Add 6 chittacks*
of sugar or 1 seer* if you intend to keep it
for a long time. Boil together with a piece
of cinnamon until the syrup is thick.

Guava Marmalade

Ingredients

Method

Guavas
Sugar
Lime juice

Strain the pulp of 100 guavas through a
piece of net. Add 1 seer* or a little more
of sugar according to taste. Add a wine
glass of lime juice. Cook over a fire,
stirring all the while, till the juice dries.

(Editor's note: 100 seems to be a lucky
number in Anglo Indian recipes).

Guava Jelly

Ingredients

Guavas

Method

100 guavas (I told you) cut into slices. Put as much water as will cover it and boil on a brisk fire till the guavas are quite soft.

Tie them in a duster and let the juice drip out. Cook on a brisk fire till it is the consistency of honey.

Pineapple Jelly

Ingredients

Pineapples
Salt
Sugar

Method

4 pineapples peeled. Rub with salt and wash nicely. Cut into small cubes. Add 1 seer* of sugar and cook over a slow fire till transparent.

Home-made Marmalade

Ingredients

2 lbs oranges
1 lb lemons
6 pints water
6 lbs sugar

Method

Wash the fruit and slice finely. Remove the pips and peel and tie in a piece of muslin. They are retained to give a stronger flavour and help to set the marmalade.

Put the fruit and bag of pips into a bowl with the water and soak overnight. This softens the peel but may be omitted if time is limited.

Put into a preserving pan and simmer gently for ½ hour until the peel is tender and the contents of the pan is reduced to half.

Remove the pips, squeezing the bag against the side of the pan with a wooden spoon to save the juice.

Add the sugar, either granulated, lumps or preserving sugar. Stir until dissolved then boil briskly.

Let the marmalade cool slightly so that the peel will be suspended, if shred marmalade is required. Put into clean warmed jars at once and cover.

Home made Marmalade.

(Mrs Manns)

2 lbs oranges, 1 lbs lemons, 6 pints water
6 lbs sugar.

(1) Wash the fruits slice finely.

(2) Remove the pips & pith, & tie in a piece of muslin. They are retained to give a stronger flavour & help to set the marmalade.

(3) put the fruit & bag of pips into a bowl with the water & soak over night. This softens the peel. but may be omitted if time is limited

(4) Put into a preserving pan and simmer gently for 1½ hours until the peel is tender and the contents of the pan reduced by half

(5) Remove the pips. squeezing the bag against the side of the pan with a wooden spoon to remove the juice.

(6) Add the sugar. either granulated, lump preserving sugar, stir until dissolved then boil briskly.

(7) Test for a set. by putting a little of the marmalade in a cool saucer, leaving it to cool & wrinkling your finger

(8) Let the marmalade cool slightly so that the peel will suspended, if a shred marmalade is required.

(9) Put into clean warmed jars at once, cover with wax

Grandmother's Home-made Marmalade recipe circa 1900

83

NOTES

_____

_____

_____

_____

_____

_____

_____

DESSERTS

Lemon Fritters

Ingredients

3 tbsp of ground
   breadcrumbs
2 tbsp of suet
2 tbsps of sugar
2 tsps of flour
2 eggs
1 lemon, juice
and rind

Method

Mix the breadcrumbs and suet together.
Then the sugar and flour. The eggs must
be well beaten and if needed a spoonful
of milk may be added.

Lastly add the rind and juice of the lemon.
Fry the mixture in small fritters.

Meringue

Ingredients

2 chittacks* of
    sugar
2 egg whites

Method

Beat the whites of the eggs with the
sugar which must be pounded. This makes
6 meringues.

Rusk Pudding

Ingredients

Custard
Rusks
Butter
Sugar
Stoned prunes

Method

Make half a pint of custard and pour it
while hot over a couple of rusks in a small
pie dish. Beat with a fork. Flavour to taste.
Place a few bits of butter and bake till a
nice brown. Serve with sifted sugar and
prunes stoned.

Nomcara Pudding

Ingredients

4 oz suet
4 oz currants
4 oz raisins
4 oz flour
4 tsp treacle
½ pint milk
Breadcrumbs
A pinch of salt

Method

Shred the suet. Clean and stalk the currants and stalk and half the raisins. Sift the flour with the breadcrumbs and salt. Warm the treacle on the fire.

Mix the ingredients all together and stir in the treacle and lastly pour in the milk teasing it in with a wooden spoon. Put it in a greased basin and steam or boil for 4 hours.

Almond Pudding

Ingredients

3 oz flour
3 oz butter
3 oz castor sugar
2 eggs
Almond flavouring

Method

Beat butter and sugar until creamy and smooth. Beat the yolks and whites of the eggs separately. Add yolks to the butter and sugar. Sift in the flour. Add the stiffly whisked whites.

Mix quickly and add a few drops of flavouring. Pour into small teacups, half filled.

Bake in a not too hot oven for 25 minutes. Turn out on a warm plate and place a piece of sweetened butter on top of each piece. If liked, some jam sauce can be substituted for the butter.

Chocolate Sponge Pudding

Ingredients

2 oz butter
2 ozs ground rice
I tsp baking powder
2 eggs
2 oz sugar
2 oz flour
2 oz cocoa
1 tsp vanilla
Salt

Method

Mix flour and cocoa together and put through a fine sieve. Cream the butter and sugar and add the eggs well beaten. Sift in the flour, cocoa and salt little by little and add 1 tablespoon of milk.

Do not let the mixture be too moist but just enough to drop thickly from a spoon. Add the vanilla and pour into a greased cake tin. Cover with greased paper and steam for 2 hours.

Turn and pour a custard round it and place halves of glace cherries or candied fruit at regular intervals on the top. With a little trouble, this may be made almost lovely "party sweet" if cooked in a fancy mould and the custard coloured with cochineal. It is very attractive.

Blanched almonds should be stuck all through it and cherries or violets used as decorations. The custard needs to be rather thick and highly flavoured and if the cochineal is dropped in and the spoon stirred only once, a very pretty marbled effect is gained.

Blackberry Semolina

Ingredients

1 tin blackberry
  puree
2 pints water
4 oz semolina

Method

Warm the blackberry juice and mix the semolina and stir well. Cook for 10 minutes over a low fire.

Cool lightly then whip hard until frothy. Cool and serve with mock cream or ice cream.

Junket*

Ingredients

1 pint milk
Nutmeg
1 tsp essence of
  rennet
1 tsp sugar

Method

Warm the milk to blood heat and sugar and rennet. Mix a little and stand to set for 1 or 2 hours.

Fresh Rice Pudding

Ingredients

3 oz sugar
3 oz rice
3 oz suet
4 oz raisins
3 oz candied peel
2 eggs
1 pint milk

Method

Wash the rice several times. Put it into the saucepan with the milk and let it cook till the milk is absorbed. Stone and chop the raisins and chop the suet. Slice the peel. Mix all with the rice. Steam for 2 hours.

Fruit Pudding

Ingredients

Suet crust
Fresh fruit
Sugar

Method

Make the suet crust and cut off ¼. Line a greased pudding basin with it. Fill with prepared fruit and sugar.

Roll a small piece to a round. Damp the edges and place over the fruit and twist over the edge.

Tie over it a damp plain cloth and boil for 2½ hours or longer. Turn out on a hot dish.

Xmas Pudding

Ingredients

1 lb suet
1 lb raisins
1 lb currants
½ lb sultanas
½ lb candied peel
4 lbs breadcrumbs
8 eggs
½ pint milk
1 lb brown sugar
½ teaspoon salt
A teaspoon mixed
    spices
Rind of 2 lemons

Method

Mix all well together. Tie up in a cloth which has been well floured and boil for 3 ½ to 4 hours.

(Editor's note "Wot!! No Brandy?)

Banana Whisk

Ingredients

8/9 ripe bananas
A packet of lemon
   jelly
Jug of whipped
   cream
Sugar to taste
A few drops of
vanilla to taste and
about 4 drops of
cochineal

Method

The lemon jelly should be made several hours a the day before it is required for use. Peel the bananas and mash them and pass through a sieve. Add the lemon jelly and whisk together briskly. Add the whipped cream and sugar to taste.

Add half a teaspoon of vanilla and cochineal and whisk again until light. Pour into a large glass or separate small glasses and decorate with crystallised fruit.

Lady Pudding

Ingredients

2 chittacks* butter
2 chittacks* sugar
2 chittacks* flour
Yolks & whites of 4
   eggs
6 sweet almonds
   pounded
The grated rind of a
lemon

Method

Beat the butter to a cream, add the flour and sugar. Beat the yolks and whites of the eggs separately. Add the pounded almonds and lemon.

Beat all together and half fill some small cups, which must be buttered inside. Set in a warm place for 5 minutes to rise and bake for half an hour.

Ginger Pudding (1)

Ingredients

½ pint milk
6 sponge cakes
Eggs
6 oz preserved
　ginger
1 tsp syrup
Butter

Method

Take 6 sponge cakes. Soak them in ½ pint of milk. Add the yolks of 4 eggs (beaten), 6 ounces preserved ginger cut into small pieces, 1 teaspoon of syrup and 1 ounce of melted butter.

Mix well and pour into a buttered dish and boil for 45 minutes.

Ginger Pudding (2)

Ingredients

1½ pints sweet
　boiled milk
8 oz grated bread
2 oz flour
6 oz butter
6 eggs
8 oz dried
preserved gingor
custard

Method

Pour 1 ½ pints of sweet boiled milk over eight ounces of grated bread and 2 ounces of flour Beat six ounces of fresh butter to a cream, then beat 1 egg, beat for a little, then take another egg and so on till you have added six.

Mince eight ounces of dried preserved ginger and when the bread and milk are quite cold beat till smooth and mix all together.

Butter a fancy mould. Cut out small pieces of angelica of various designs and stick them to the mould, then pour in the pudding and boil for 2 hours.

Serve with custard all around it. Half of the ingredients given in this recipe will make a good sized pudding.

Date Pudding (1)

Ingredients

¾ lbs of breadcrumbs
6 oz of finely chopped suet
¼ lb of chopped dates
3 ounces moist sugar
2 eggs beaten
Half a cup of milk

Method

Mix the breadcrumbs and suet together. Then add the remainder of the ingredients. Mix together. Boil for an hour.

Date Pudding (2)

Ingredients

¼ lbs of breadcrumbs
¼ lbs of flour
¼ lbs of sugar
¼ lbs of chopped suet
½ dates
¼ tsp bicarbonate of soda
Egg
Butter/milk

Method

Mix together a quarter of a pound of breadcrumbs with an equal amount of flour, sugar and finely chopped suet.

Add half a pound of dates cut into small pieces and a quarter teaspoon of bicarbonate of soda and mix all together. Beat an egg and stir it in it. Add enough butter, milk or skimmed milk to make a thick batter.

Pour it all into a buttered mould or pudding basin. The butter must not be too thin or the dates will possibly stick to the bottom of the mould or pudding basin. Cover it with well-buttered paper and steam for 2 ½ hours.

Apple Pudding

Ingredients

1 lb of apples
3 oz sugar
6 oz self-raising
   flour
Pinch of salt
1 level teaspoon
   ground spices
1 ½ teacups milk
   and water
½ tsp lemon
essence

Method

Sift flour, salt and spices and rub in fat
then mix in 1/2 ounces of sugar. Beat in
half the liquid smoothly and gradually.
Beat thoroughly till bubbles appear, then
mix in the rest of the liquid and the
lemon essence.

Peel and core the apples and cut into small
pieces and mix with 2 ounces sugar. Put in
a greased Pyrex dish and pour the batter
over it. Bake in a moderate oven for 45
minutes or an hour until golden brown.
Sprinkle with the rest of the sugar and
serve hot.

Boiled Apple Pudding

Ingredients

½ lb flour
5 oz suet
½ tsp baking
powder
Salt
Water
Apples
Cloves

Method

Make a suet crust. Line a basin. Put in
apples and cloves and boil for 1½ hours.

Apple Dumplings

Ingredients

4 oz flour
Pinch of salt
2 oz butter
Cold water for
 mixing
1 tsp brown sugar
4 apples
2 cloves to each
apple

Method

Make the short crust pastry. Peel and
core the apples. Divide the pastry into 4
pieces. Roll out each piece into a round
sufficiently large enough to enclose the
apples. Turn the pieces over so that rolled
side is next to the board.

Place the apples on the piece of pastry. Fill
the centre of the apples with the sugar and
cloves. Close the edge of the pastry and
work the pastry round the apple until it is
quite covered sealing the edge well.

Place on a greased tin and bake for
30 minutes.

Venice Pudding

Ingredients

4 tbsp of flour
Milk
2 tbsp of sugar
1 egg
Jam
½ oz butter
I tsp of baking
powder

Method

Rub butter in the flour. Add sugar and a
pinch of salt and baking powder. Mix well
all through.

Beat up eggs and pour into it a cup of milk
and mix well with the other ingredients.
Stir into a smooth batter (if too stiff add
milk). Butter a pudding dish. Put a layer
of batter, then a layer of jam and the rest
of the batter. Bake in hot oven and test if
ready after 1/2 hour.

Rhubarb and Syrup Pudding

Ingredients

8 oz of self-raising
   flour
½ lb of rhubarb
2 oz syrup
2 oz of sugar
Fat
Milk and water
to mix

Method

Cut up the rhubarb in small pieces. Mix
the fat into the dry ingredients and add the
milk and water to make a stiff paste. Add
the rhubarb. Place in a well-greased basin
and steam for 2 and a half hours. Serve
with custard.

Rhubarb Snow

Ingredients

1 lb rhubarb
3 oz syrup
2 tbsp water
1 ½ tbsp semolina
½ pint of milk
1 tsp sugar
A few drops of
lemon essence

Method

Cut the rhubarb into small pieces and
cook very gently with the syrup and 2
tablespoons until pulpy. Mix semolina with
the milk and water. Bring to a boil stirring
all the time and cook for 10 minutes.

Add the rhubarb pulp and lemon essence
and turn into a basin to cool.

When cold, but not set, beat until light
and frothy. If liked, pile in individual glass
dishes. Sprinkle with sugar or jam.

Chocolate Suet Pudding

Ingredients

Method

¼ lb flour
½ oz cocoa
2 oz suet
3 oz sugar
½ tsp bicarbonate
   of soda
1 tsp vanilla
½ pint milk
1 egg

Sift the flour into a basin with the cocoa and bicarbonate of soda. Stir in the shredded suet and sugar. Beat up the eggs and add it to the milk. Mix all together and beat well, then stir in the vanilla.

Turn the mixture into a greased basin, cover with greased paper and steam till firm for 2 ½ hours. Serve with top of milk or hot custard.

Secrets of a Nice Custard Pudding

Ingredients

Method

Eggs
2 teacups milk

2 eggs beaten together. Bring 2 teacups of milk to the boil. Add the milk to the eggs (Never put the eggs to the milk).

Slow fire for ten minutes. Stir all the time.

Tinned Peaches in Stale Cake

Ingredients

Tinned peaches
Stale cake
Whipped cream
Preserved cherry

Method

Drain a tin of peaches from their juice.
Place rounds of stale cake in glass dishes
and pour a little of the peach juice on
each round of cake.

Fill the cavities of the peaches with
chopped preserved cherries. Top with
whipped sweetened cream and a
preserved cherry.

Brown Sugar Rings

Ingredients

2 egg whites
4 oz light brown
  sugar
1 oz flatted
  almonds
1 tsp coffee essence
¼ pint whipped
cream

Method

Whisk egg whites till stiff then whisk in
half sugar till smooth. Fold in remaining
sugar. Pipe 3 inch rings. Sprinkle almonds
over rings.

Bake about 1½ hours at 225 F/110C.
Then sandwich together with cream.

Ice Cream

Ingredients   Method

Condensed milk   1 tin condensed milk dissolved in hot
                               water. Cooled then put into freezer
                               and flavoured.

Bibinca

Ingredients   Method

½ seer* sugar   Put coconut cream into the hot water and
6 eggs   add sugar. Beat up eggs together and add
5 oz rice flour   with fresh milk to the coconut and sugar
½ seer* hot water   syrup and cook until thick and it leaves
1 coconut (or   the pan.
  substitute coconut
  cream)   Pour into glass dish to cool.
2 pints milk

Raisin Pie with Cheese

Ingredients

Sliced cheese
Raisins

Method

Make a raisin pie in the usual way
and place a layer of thinly sliced cheese
over the raisins, before covering with
the upper crust.

Pancakes

Ingredients

½ lb of flour
5 eggs
Milk

Method

With nearly half a pound of flour mix 5
eggs and then add, by degrees, a quart
of good milk.

Heat your pancake frying pan well. Then
drop 1 tablespoon of the batter on to this.
Serve with sugar between each.

NOTES

_____

_____

_____

_____

_____

_____

_____

CAKES

Swiss Rolls

Ingredients

Method

Eggs
Flour
Milk
Sugar

The weight of 2 eggs in sugar and 1 of flour. Put the sugar in a basin with the yolks. Stir well till very smooth.

Whip the whites and add to the mixture and lastly the flour. Put at once into a tin lined with greased paper.

Bake in a hot oven for 8 minutes. Have ready a sheet of paper with sugar sifted over it. Turn the roll onto this. Spread it over and roll up quickly.

Genuine Sponge Cake

Ingredients

Method

4 eggs
2/3 of a cup of sugar
2/3 cup of lemon
   juice
Grate rind of the
   lemon
¼ teaspoon of salt

Beat the yolks of the eggs till they thicken and get creamy. Add the sugar a little at a time, beating with an egg beater.

Add lemon juice and grated rind. Beat the white of the eggs till stiff. When the whites are partly mixed with the yolks and sugar, add flour and the salt. Mix and bake for 1 hour over a low flame.

Walnut Cake

Ingredients

Method

1 ¼ lb flour
1 oz baking powder
8 oz sugar
8 oz butter
½ tsp vanilla
2 ½ oz of walnuts

Cream the butter and sugar. Add the
eggs and beat well. Stir in the flour, milk,
vanilla and chopped walnuts.

Icing for Walnut Cake

Ingredients

Method

1 ½ lbs loaf sugar
½ pint water
3 whites of eggs

Melt the sugar in the water and allow it to
boil till quite thick and big bubbles. Put
it into the eggs which have been beaten
to a very stiff froth. Put over the cake and
decorate it with walnuts.

Cream Tea Cakes

Ingredients

8 oz butter
16 oz flour
4 oz sugar
4 eggs
1 tsp baking powder
1 pint thick sour
cream

Method

Rub 8 ounces of butter into 16 ounces of flour. Make a well into the centre into which put 4 ounces of sugar and 4 eggs. Now add a teaspoonful of baking powder. Throw in a pint of thick sour cream.

Mix the whole quickly into a paste. Roll very lightly. Mould into rounds and bake in a brisk oven.

Shrewsbury Cakes

Ingredients

½ lb of fresh butter
Rose water
Flour
7 oz pounded loaf
Sugar
2 eggs
Caraway seeds

Method

Mix with half a pound of fresh butter, washed in rose water and beaten to a cream. The same quantity of dried and sifted flour. Seven ounces of pounded loaf sugar. Half a teaspoon of caraway seeds. And 2 well beaten eggs.

Make into a paste. Roll it thin. Cut it into round cakes. Prick them and bake them in floured tins.

Sponge Cake

Ingredients

12 eggs
20 oz lump sugar
Wine glass of water
16 oz sifted flour
Juice of half a
lemon

Method

Always grease tins with mutton fat before putting the mixture in. Grease sponge tins and while warm sift castor sugar over it.

Put the lump sugar in a saucepan with water and when the sugar is quite melted (not brown) add it to the eggs in a large bowl. Mix for 20 minutes or until mixture is thick and creamy, fold in the flour. Mix and add in the lemon juice. Put in the tins and sprinkle more sugar on the top. Bake in a moderately hot oven for an hour or more. When the baking is done, it will leave the side of the tin.

Queen Cakes

Ingredients

1 egg
Butter
Sugar
Flour
1/8 tsp baking
  powder
Grated lemon rind
½ oz currants

Method

Grease 6 or 8 tins with clarified butter. Cream the butter and sugar. Beat in the egg. Sieve the flour and sift it in lightly mixing the baking powder with the last teaspoon. Add the prepared fruit and half fill the tins. Bake in the oven for 20 minutes.

Christmas Cake (1)

Ingredients

2 lbs butter
½ lb brown sugar
½ lb raisins
1 ¼ lb mixed fruit
½ lb sliced and ½
  lb crushed
  almonds
½ lb flour
½ lb sujee*
20 eggs
½ tsp vanilla
  essence
½ tsp almond
  essence
½ tsp cinnamon
¼ lb double cream
Wine glass full
brandy

Method

Mix egg yolks and sugar until creamy.
Add butter, cinnamon, almond essence,
vanilla essence and mix well.

Then mix sujee*, flour, mix fruits and add
gradually with the cream well mixed and
add to all the mixture. Beat the egg whites
and "fold" in with the brandy last of all.

Put into two 12 inch tins and bake for 2
hours. Makes nearly 10 lbs of cake.

Christmas Cake (2)

Ingredients

1 lb unsalted butter
12 oz white sugar
1 lb raisins and/or
  sultanas
8 oz whole almonds
2 oz orange peel
12 oz self-raising
  flour
4 oz semolina
6 eggs
Brandy

Method

Mix sugar, eggs yolks, add butter, flour,
semolina and glazed preserves. Beat
whites of eggs till stiff. Add brandy and
mix well. Cook at 150c.

Christmas Cake (3)

Ingredients

½ lb butter
4 oz brown sugar
½ lb raisins and/or
sultanas
4 oz whole almonds
1 oz orange Citroën
4 oz self-raising
flour
4 oz semolina
3 or 4 eggs
Brandy

Method

Mix sugar and yolk of eggs, add butter, then flour and semolina, then balance of preserves. Beat whites of eggs and mix in brandy to ingredients. (Or pour brandy over top of the cake when cooked).
Bake for 3 hours 150c.

Icing for cakes

Ingredients

4 tbs sugar
2 tbs milk/water
Cream of tatar
Sugar

Method

Put 4 tablespoons of sugar in a saucepan with 2 tablespoons of milk or water. A pinch of cream of tartar. Melt the sugar and bring it to a boil for 1 minute only.

Almond Rice Cake

Ingredients

2 cups of sugar
½ cup of butter
2 ½ teacups of
    flour (measured
    after sifting 5
    times)
¾ of a cup of milk
Whites of 6 eggs
1 lb of almonds
    weighed with the
    shells
1 tsp of baking
    powder
1 tsp of almond
essence

Method

Cream the butter and sugar and beat for 5 minutes until frothy. Then add flour into which baking powder has been sifted. Add slowly three quarters of a cup of milk a little at a time.

Shell blanch and chop the almonds and add to the other ingredients. Lastly the whites of the eggs well beaten and the essence of almonds.

Put into deep sandwich tins and bake in a quick oven for about 35 to 40 minutes.

When done and quite hot, spread over the top a very thin layer of melted jelly and sprinkle with brown and chopped almonds. (Use only sufficient jelly to make the almonds stick).

Orange Cake

Ingredients

¾ of a cup of butter
1 ¼ cups of sugar
Yolks of 6 eggs
½ cup of milk
1 ½ cups of flour
    sifted
1 tsp of baking
    powder
Orange colouring

Method

Proceed in the same way with the mixing as in the recipe for the Almond Rice Cake (above). Put half the mixture into a sandwich tin and into the remaining half put a few drops of orange colouring. Bake in a good hot oven.

(Editor's note: orange colouring can be replaced by orange rind for a healthier option and the cake topped with glazed slices of orange, see photograph p.103).

Rock Cake

Ingredients

8 oz flour
2 oz currants
½ tsp baking
   powder
2 oz butter
2 oz sugar
1 oz candied peel
A little milk
½ tsp salt
Grated lemon rind
Egg

Method

Rub butter into flour and add the sugar, baking powder, peel and currants. Beat the egg. Add the grated lemon and a little milk to make stiff dough.

Place on a baking sheet. Prick with a fork and bake at once.

Ground Rice Cakes

Ingredients

¾ breakfast cupful
   ground rice
4 eggs and same
   weight in sugar
¼ tsp lemon
essence

Method

Beat yolks and whites of the eggs separately. Beat the sugar and yolks then add the whites. Then beat in the flour. Bake for 45 minutes.

Adelaide Cake

Ingredients

3 oz of cornflour
½ oz flour
3 oz butter
3 oz sugar
3 eggs
3 oz flour
½ tsp vanilla
essence

Method

Beat the butter and sugar to a cream.
Beat up the eggs. Sift the 3 flours well
together. Add them to the sugar and butter,
alternately with the eggs, which have been
beaten to a stiff froth.

Then add the vanilla and a little milk.
Bake in well-buttered tins for twenty
minutes. When ready leave for an hour
or so till quite cool.

Eclairs

Ingredients

Choux pastry with 2
ounces flour
½ pint whipped
cream or crème
Chantilly
(opposite)
2 oz coffee glace
icing

Method

Prepare oven 200°C and make choux
pastry (see p.127).

Bake without opening oven door until set
and firm when they should be well risen,
brown and hollow inside.

Slit down one side and, if necessary, put
back in the oven to dry off completely.
When quite cold fill with crème Chantilly
and ice tops with glace icing.

Time taking about 30 minutes.
Makes about 8 eclairs.

Crème Chantilly

Ingredients	Method
¼ pint double cream ½ oz icing sugar Vanilla essence	Sieve icing sugar. Half whip cream. Add sugar and essence and continue to whip until desired consistency, taking care not to over whip when cream will become buttery.

Crème Patisserie

Ingredients	Method
1 egg (separated) 1 rounded tab castor sugar 1 tbsp flour ¼ pint milk 2 to 3 drops vanilla essence	Cream egg yolk and sugar together. Fold in the flour. Stir in the milk to give a smooth even texture. Bring slowly to boil, stirring well, and allow to boil for 2/3 minutes. Fold in stiffly whisked egg white, bring just to boil, folding mixture in carefully. Cool and stir in vanilla essence and spoonful of top of milk or cream.

Glace Icing for Éclairs

Ingredients	Method
2 oz icing sugar 1 tsp coffee 1 dessertspoon water	Sieve sugar and put in basin over a pan of warm water. Add coffee and water. Stir gently over heat until icing is smooth. Do not overheat.

Chocolate Potato Cake

Ingredients

Method

2 cupful flour
3 eggs
1 orange
½ tsp salt
4 tsp baking powder
4 cupful sugar
Salt
½ Nutmeg (grated)
1 tsp cinnamon
½ cup butter
1 cupful hot mashed
  potatoes
Lemon Juice
½ cup hot milk
½ oz cocoa or
  chocolate
Icing sugar

Beat butter and sugar to a cream. Add 1
well beaten egg, then stir in the potatoes
which should have been passed through a
masher till quite light and smooth.

Sift salt, baking powder, flour, cinnamon
and nutmeg together. Add to butter and
sugar alternately with hot milk in which
the cocoa has been dissolved. Bake in two
small buttered cake tins and when cold,
spread with orange icing.

Let the grated rind of 1 orange soak
in the juice squeezed out for ½ hour.
Stir in lightly beaten yolks of 2 eggs,
2 teaspoons of lemon juice and enough
icing sugar to make icing spreadable.

Welsh Cheese Cakes

Ingredients

¼ lb pastry
Equal weight of
   butter, sugar
   and flour
1 egg
1 tsp of baking
   powder
Jam

Method

Line pastry pans with pastry. Put in a little jam, then some of the mixture. Bake in a hot oven then a moderate oven for 20 minutes to half hour.

NOTES

_____

_____

_____

_____

_____

_____

_____

BISCUITS, SCONES & DOUGHNUTS

Scones

Ingredients

2 tbsp of sugar
2 eggs beaten
1 tsp of baking
   powder
1 of fine sifted flour
A pinch of salt
About a cup of milk

Method

Mix together the eggs and sugar, add the milk and put in the flour.

Mix to a rough paste and cut out with a glass and bake in the oven which should not be too hot.

Buttermilk Scones

Ingredients

1 ½ breakfast cups
   flour
¾ breakfast cup
   buttermilk
1 dessert spoon
   butter
1 dessert spoonful
   baking powder
2 tsp of sugar
1 egg and a pinch
of salt

Method

Break egg and drop it into dish containing butter and sugar. The mixture may appear slightly clotted but it is immaterial. Add ¾ breakfast cup of buttermilk and mix.

In a bowl mix baking powder and flour. Add to the bowl of baking powder and flour, the other mixture containing egg, sugar, butter and buttermilk. Lightly mix together with fingers.

If slightly too dry, add just sufficient buttermilk to it but be careful not to add too much. Turn out of bowl on floured board and shape into round flat bits and bake on greased tins for 15 minutes. Makes 12 scones.

Biscuits

Ingredients

1 seer* of flour
3 chittacks * butter
2 tsp of bicarbonate
   of soda
Treacle as required
½ oz of bisque
oxide of iron

Method

Mix the flour, soda and sift well together
then rub in the butter. Then add as much
treacle as when worked will make a stiff
dough. Allow this to stand for 24 hours.

Cut out and divide into 12 dozen biscuits.
Bake in the oven. Each biscuit contains
about 1 ½ grams of oxide of iron.

Shortbread

Ingredients

3 oz sugar
3 oz butter
10 oz flour
Egg

Method

The sugar to be sifted and mixed with the
flour. Butter to be added. Last of all the
egg to be put in and kneaded for a little
while. Bake in a good oven.

Oatmeal Biscuits

Ingredients

Method

5 oz flour
7 oz oatmeal
1 oz sugar
4 oz butter
2 eggs
¼ tsp of
bicarbonate of soda

Sieve flour, add oatmeal, sugar and soda.
Mix well and mix them with the melted fat
(butter) and beaten eggs. Knead lightly
into a dough. Roll out and cut into rounds.
Bake for ¼ hour.

Macaroons (1)

Ingredients

Method

¼ lb pounded
    almonds
Egg
½ lb of sifted sugar
Powdered sugar

¼ lb blanched and pounded almonds, wet
them with the white of an egg to prevent
them being oily. Mix ½ lb of sifted sugar
with white of an egg. Add the almonds
and mix.

Lay them on a paper or tin rather thin and
bake in a moderate oven. When done,
shake some powdered sugar over them
through a sieve.

Macaroons (2)

Ingredients

Method

1 lb sugar
1 lb almonds or
    coconut grated
Eggs

Mix a pound of sugar and a pound of
almonds or coconut grated. Mix with stiffly
beaten whites of eggs.

Make biscuits and bake in a moderate
oven. Pounded almond or sugar may be
sprinkled over the macaroons.

Pineapple and Coconut Fingers

Ingredients

½ lb flour
4 oz margarine
1 egg
1 level teaspoon
  baking powder

Topping:
2 rounded tbsp jam
4 pineapple rings
  crushed
4 oz coconut
3 oz sugar
1 oz margarine
1 egg
A rectangular tin 12
by 8 inches

Method

Brush the inside of the tin very thoroughly with fat. Sieve the flour and the baking powder. Rub the margarine into the flour. Beat the eggs and gradually work into the mixture.

Press the pastry into the base of the tin with your fingers and using a palette knife spread the mixture thinly with the jam and arrange the pineapple.

Rub the margarine into the coconut and sugar. Beat the eggs and add to the mixture. Spread this mixture evenly over the pastry.

Bake in a moderate oven till done. Cut into equal slices and, when cold, remove from tin.

Tea Biscuits

Ingredients

1 cup sugar
8 oz butter
2 eggs
½ tsp vanilla
3 ¼ cups flour

Method

Cream butter and sugar. Add eggs and vanilla. Beat thoroughly and add flour gradually. Mix until smooth. Form into fancy shapes and bake in hot oven for 6 minutes.

Normandy Puffs

Ingredients

Butter
1 breakfast cup of
  flour
1 chittack* of white
  sugar
1 tsp essence of
  vanilla
Eggs

Method

Take a piece of butter the size of an egg
and mix it into a breakfast cup of flour.
Add a breakfast cupful of boiling water.
1 chittack* of white sugar. 1 teaspoon
essence of vanilla and 4 eggs each one
separately added to the mixture.

Mix well and leave in a cool place for
3 hours. Drop dessertspoonfuls of the
mixture in hot butter and fry.

Doughnuts

Ingredients

½ lb of flour
1 heaped tsp of
  baking powder
A pinch of salt
1 tbs sugar
Butter
Egg
Buttermilk

Method

Sift these well together. Add a tablespoon
of sugar and rub in a good size piece of
butter. Make a hole in the centre of the
mixture and drop in an egg.

Add as much butter milk as would make a
stiff dough. Drop in a teaspoon at a time
into boiling fat and when light brown,
drain on paper and dust with sifted sugar.

Golabjamons

Ingredients

4 tbsp milk
4 oz full cream
    powdered milk
1 level tablespoon
    flour
1 level tablespoon
    sujee*
1 lb sugar
Pinch of
bicarbonate
    of soda
Cardamoms crushed
Oil for frying

Method

Mix dry milk, flour, sujee and bicarbonate
in a bowl. Add milk to make smooth
soft dough.

Dissolve sugar with half pint water on low
fire. Keep on a very low fire while frying.
Make dough into small balls (they swell out
later). Fry in oil and when nice and brown,
drop into boiling syrup. Cover and allow
to stand for at least 24 hours.

NOTES

_____

_____

_____

_____

_____

_____

_____

PASTRY

Pastry

Ingredients

12 chittacks* flour
8 chittacks* butter
6 chittacks* fine
   sugar
4 eggs

Method

Mix the sugar and butter well. Add the
flour and eggs. Turn out on to a floured
board and cut into pastry pieces.

Flaky Pastry

Ingredients

8 oz flour
3 oz butter
3 oz lard
Pinch of salt

Method

Sieve salt and flour into a basin. Divide
the butter and lard into 2 pieces. Roll out
and then mix to a stiff paste with water.
Roll out the paste to a strip. Spread half
the lard in flakes over 2/3 of the paste and
dredge very lightly with flour.

Fold the pastry in threes with the plain
part in the centre. Seal the edge of the
folded pastry. Half fold the pastry to bring
the folded edge to the side. Roll the pastry
to a strip being careful not to roll over the
top and bottom edge as the air folded in
would be expelled. Repeat this for 6 to 10
times using the remainder of the butter.
Repeat from 6 to 10 times but this time no
fat is used. When the pastry has thus been
rolled and folded four times roll it out as
required. Bake in a hot oven.

Choux Pastry

Ingredients

2 oz flour
2 eggs
1 oz butter
½ gill* water
Salt

Method

Heat a small pan of hot water with the butter to a boiling point. Stir in the sieved flour and some salt and cook serving well until mixture forms soft balls of dough, leaving the sides of the pan.

Remove from heat, cool and beat in the egg a little at a time. Cool and use as required.

NOTES

_____

_____

_____

_____

_____

_____

_____

SWEETS

Doldol

Ingredients

Method

2 coconuts
2 cups sugar
Few cardamoms
1 ½ or 2 chittacks*
rice flour

Scrape the coconuts and put into 3 cups of boiling water, cover and stand for 15 minutes. Then put into a strong jharan* and take out the milk. To this add the sugar and flour. Stir well so that all lumps are well mixed.

Put on a slow fire and cook gently, stirring all the time until quite thick and the sides leave the pan. A few cardamoms must be added.

Sugared Almonds

Ingredients

Method

2 lbs almonds
1 tbs salad oil
1 tsp sugar

Blanch about 2 lbs of almonds and pour over them a tablespoon of salad oil. Let them stand in this for a couple of hours. Then add a teaspoonful of sugar.

Shake them about and then brown them in the oven.

Italian and French Nougat

Ingredients

½ lb icing sugar
3 whites of eggs
¼ lb honey
1 tbsp glucose (may
  be omitted)
½ lb chopped fruit
  and nuts
Rice or wafer paper

Method

Put icing sugar in a pan and stand the pan in another of boiling water until the sugar is quite dissolved. Add the glucose and the eggs beaten to a froth. Stir all together well and then test in cold water.

When the mixture can be pulled into threads, it is done. Add fruit and remove from the boiling water and stir till almost cold. Turn out on an oiled slab or tin and shape into a square piece about 1 or 1 ½ inches thick, placing a piece of rice paper on top and bottom. Leave it till firm and set and then cut into pieces.

Marzipan

Ingredients

1 lb lump or good
  white sugar
1 tea cup water
12 oz ground
  almonds
2 whites of eggs (or
1 whole egg)

Method

Boil sugar and water together without stirring until it forms threads when pressed between the thumb and the finger. (This can be done by lifting out a couple of drops on a spoon). Add the almonds and eggs.

Cook for another few minutes then turn out on a slab and knead slightly, using a little icing sugar to flour the fingers.

Barley Sugar Candy

Ingredients

1 lb loaf sugar
½ pint water
Juice of a lemon or
  lime
A pinch of cream of
  tartar
A few drops of
essence of lemon

Method

Let the sugar dissolve slowly in the water
and the allow it to boil. Skim off any scum
that may arise but the mixture must not be
stirred. Boil to 300 degrees. Now add the
juice and essence and allow the sugar to
come to the boil again.

Pour the mixture onto a oiled tin or slab
and as the mixture cools, cut off strips the
size of a finger commencing at the edge.
Roll them in the form of round sticks and
twist, so as to resemble a corkscrew.
Allow them to harden on a greased tin
and store in a well stoppered jar. A little
saffron or cochineal may be added to give
it a colour.

Turkish Delight

Ingredients

1 lb loaf sugar
1 teacup water
Juice of a lemon
¼ tbsp rose water
1 oz French leaf
  gelatine
A few drops of
  cochineal
Icing sugar

Method

Dissolve the gelatine in water and add the
lemon juice and sugar. Let the ingredients
dissolve slowly and then boil quickly for
5 minutes.

Add the rose water and put half the
mixture into an oiled tin. Colour the other
half and put into another half.

When cold turn both out. Cut into small
blocks and roll each piece in icing sugar.

Nestles Milk and Coconut Milk Toffee

Ingredients

1 ½ lb of sugar
1 tin Nestles milk
¼ lb butter
Coconut

Method

Boil sugar and milk together for 15 minutes, then add a quarter pound of butter. Add milk that has been squeezed out of a good cocoanut after it has been shredded.

Cook together until the toffee is a pale brown shade. Cut into squares before it is quite cool.

Pistachio Nut Toffee

Ingredients

1 seer* milk
1 large breakfast
cup of pistachios
1 breakfast cup
pounded sugar
1 chattack* butter

Method

Boil 1 seer* milk till it reaches half. Add 1 large breakfast cup full of pistachios, pasted and sliced, 1 cup of pounded sugar and 1 chattack* of butter.

Boil the whole on a slow fire until when dropped into cold water it becomes crisp. Pour into a well- buttered dish and cut. The same kind of toffee can be made with ground nuts but 2 cups of sugar could be used instead of one.

Walnut Toffee

Ingredients

Method

4 lbs Golden Syrup
2 lbs walnuts
¼ tsp bicarbonate
   of soda
2 tbsp glucose

Break up the kernels of the walnuts
and mix them with the soda. Bring the
syrup and glucose gently to the boil in
a saucepan. Let it boil for a few minutes
and test by dropping into cold water. If it
hardens, take the pan off the fire and stir
in the walnuts.

Pour on buttered plates and cut into pieces
before it is quite cold.

Parkin

Ingredients

Method

12 oz medium
   oatmeal
4 oz margarine or
   lard
4 oz treacle
4 oz flour
1 tsp ground ginger
About ½ gill* milk
   or water
½ tsp of
   bicarbonate of
   soda
Grated lemon rind
   or candied peel
4 oz Golden Syrup
2 ½ oz brown sugar

Mix oatmeal, flour, peel and ginger. Heat
treacle, syrup, fat and sugar. Mix it with
the oatmeal and mix thoroughly. Mix with a
little milk. Then add all milk. And mix well.

Spread the mixture on a greased tin
and bake for 1 to 1 ½ hours on a
moderate oven.

Chocolate Toffee (1)

Ingredients

4 dessert spoons of
   grated chocolate
   or cocoa
1 breakfast cup of
   milk
2 cups of sugar
2 ½ of chittacks* of
   butter or ghee*
1 tsp of vanilla
essence

Method

Mix all together in a clean saucepan and
let it boil and stir. Pour in a well buttered
dish and cut when cool.

Chocolate Toffee (2)

Ingredients

4 dsp cocoa
1 breakfast cup
water
2 cups sugar
Vanilla essence to
   taste
½ tsp cream of
tartar

Method

Mix all together in a saucepan and boil
fast until like any other toffee it gets
difficult to stir and leaves the bottom of
the pan.

Take off the fire and beat for a couple
of minutes. Pour into a buttered tray or
flat dish and cut into squares before
quite cold.

Coconut Toffee

Ingredients

2 coconuts
1 breakfast cup milk
2 breakfast cups
sugar

Method

To the milk of 2 coconuts add a breakfast
cup of fresh milk and 2 cups of sugar.
Put into a saucepan and cook till it leaves
the side and is thick enough to pour out
into a well-buttered dish and cut when
nearly cool.

Kul Kuls

An excellent old fashioned recipe you are sure to be delighted with.

Ingredients

1 lb soojee*
3 eggs
1 teacup thick coconut milk

Method

Knead into stiff dough. Form into shapes with the back of a fork, greasing the fork occasionally with a little butter. The shapes should be in the form of little curls. Fry in boiling ghee*.

After they have cooled, weigh the kul kuls and to every 2 pounds, allow 1 pound sugar to make a syrup. When syrup thickens and gets a bit stringy, throw in the kul kuls and mix them thoroughly till they are coated with sugar and the syrup dries.

Halwa

Ingredients

1 seer* water
1 seer* sugar
3 chittacks* ghee*
½ seer* of sujee*

Method

Steep half a seer* of sujee* in 1 seer* of water for 12 hours. It will then be the milk of sujee*. Strain through a course duster, rejecting only the stuff that remained unstrained. Add to the milk of sujee* a seer of sugar. Boil it stirring all the time and as it thickens add 3 chts* of ghee*.

Continue stirring it from first to last. Take it down when quite thick and put it to set in a dish.

Suji* Halwa

Ingredients

1 lb suji*
1 lb flour
10 chittacks*
  shelled almonds
½ seer* large
  raisins (cut into
  slices)
½ seer* pumpkin
  preserve
½ seer* mixed
  preserve
½ seer* cherries
  (crystalised)
½ seer* walnuts
  (broken)
1/2 seer* ground
  almonds
2 seers* melted
  butter
2 tbsp baking
  powder
2 tsp mixed ground
  spices
1 tbsp sugar
4 eggs
1 pint rum

Method

Cut all the almonds, raisins, preserves and the rest and soak in the rum the night before baking.

Burfee

Ingredients

2 cups powdered
  milk
1 ½ cups castor
  sugar
4 tbsp water
3 ½ oz butter
4 crushed
cardamoms

Method

Mix sugar, water and cardamoms and boil for 3 minutes. Add in butter then mix into the milk. Mix well and put into flat tins and cut into square when set.

DRINKS &
HOME REMEDIES

*Marvel at these family advances in
technology and medicine brought to your
home.*

*Concoct, drink or apply entirely at your
own risk!*

Milk Punch

Ingredients

Method

3 bottles rum
1 ½ seers* sugar
20 limes – juice and
rind
2 bottles water
2 seers* milk
1 chittack* allspice*
½ chittack*
cinnamon
¼ chittack*
cardamom
1 nutmeg
8 cloves

Bruise the allspice, cinnamon and
cardamom and soak in 1 bottle of rum.
The rind and juice of the limes in another
bottle of rum. Keep in the sun for a week.

Mix all the ingredients, including the third
bottle of rum, into a large bowl with limes,
cloves, nutmeg, water and sugar and while
stirring, have the milk boiling and then
pour it gently from high, stirring all the
while for fifteen minutes.

Then cover it and leave it for 2 hours
after which strain it through a double
flannel until clear. Bottle when cool
and store in a cool place.

*(Editor's note: I just had to include this
recipe; 3 bottles of rum – makes your
eyes water).*

Hand Lotion

An inexpensive lotion for preserving hands can be made by mixing equal quantities of glycerine, milk and mentholated spirits.

Mix well together in a bottle and add a few drops of scent if liked. The lotion should be rubbed well into the hands after washing in warm water, preferably before retiring for the night.

Pomade for Falling Hair

Ingredients

8 oz of beef
   marrow
22 drops of
   cantharides
60 grams of sugar
   of lead
1 oz of spirits
   of wine
20 drops of oil of
bergamot

Method

Boil the marrow in the bone and mix the prescribed quantity free of bone and fibre with the other ingredients – excepting this scent which is added later on.

Scent. Betel nut dentifrice – the nuts should not be burnt but sliced and roasted like coffee to a rich brown colour.

Then pulverised and passed through fine muslin. Continue pounding and sifting till all is done – the colour should be a rich chocolate – tincture of myrrh camphor or eau de cologne may be added.

Remove Iron Mould

Rub the spot with a little powdered oxalic acid or salts of lemon and warm water. Leave it for a short while and then rinse in clear cold water.

Remove Stains from Dark Clothes

Boil a handful of fig leaves in 2 quarts of water until reduced to a pint. Rub on with a rag or sponge over the stains which will disappear on drying.

Indellible Marking Ink

Ingredients

2 drams Lunar
   Carnatic or Silver
   in crystals
¾ drams Tartaric
   acid in powder
1 ½ drams
   Cossipore sugar
1 oz Spirits of
   Hartshorne
2 ½ drams Gum
   Arabic powder
6 drams distilled
rain water

Method

Reduce the Nitrate of Silver to powder. Then add the sugar which is also to be powdered and lastly add the tartaric acid.

After these have been well mixed gradually stir in the Spirits of Hartshorne and pour the whole into a phial. Mix the gum with distilled water and add it to the mixture in the phial and shake it. Expose the phial to the rays of the sun for a day or two and the ink is ready to use.

N.B. A quill pen to be used. On no account a metallic one.

Iceless Freezer

An affair that comes among warm weather desirables is the machine that will give one ice cream without one getting a particle of ice wherein to produce it.

It is called a Freezovac and it functions upon a diet of carbonate of soda and nitrate of ammonia, so that should you be situated where block ice is unobtainable, all that you have to do is to lay in a stock of these chemicals in its place.

The work involved is nothing more than is represented by the turning of a handle for a couple of minutes. In twenty minutes time the ice cream will be ready for use.

The freezing mixture may, after use, be retained in a bowl for keeping siphons and bottles at a low temperature.

(Editor's note: I remember about 70 years ago, this item being a rather big wooden tub, like a small beer barrel, about 18 inches high and 10inches wide with a handle for turning. Inside was a tin like affair about 6 inches wide into with the ingredients of the ice cream was put. When it came out it was just ice cream with some small flakes of ice in it. Very useful before the advent of freezers).

NOTES

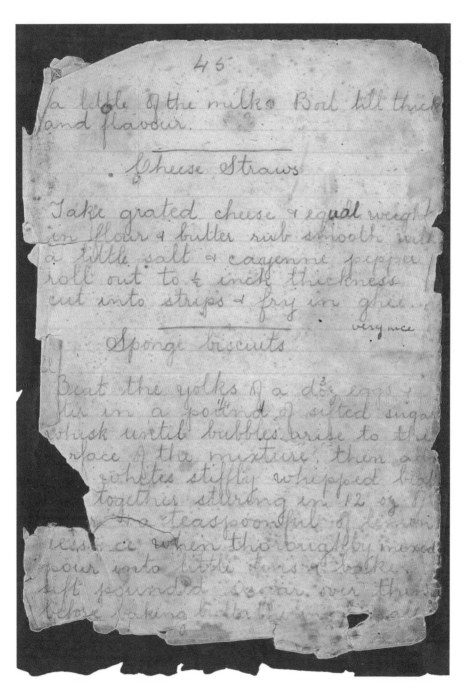

45

a little of the milk. Boil till thick and flavour.

Cheese Straws

Take grated cheese & equal weight in flour & butter rub smooth with a little salt & cayenne pepper roll out to ½ inch thickness cut into strips & fry in ghee

very nice

Sponge biscuits

Beat the yolks of a doz. eggs stir in a pound of sifted sugar whisk until bubbles arise to the surface of the mixture, then add the whites stiffly whipped beaten together stirring in 12 oz of a teaspoonful of lemon essence when thoroughly mixed pour into little tins & bake. sift pounded sugar over them before baking

Grandmother's original recipe for Cheese Straws (recipe page 19 and photographed on page 17)

NOTES

sprinkle with brown & chopped almonds
Use only sufficient jelly to make the
almonds stick. (Excellent)

Orange Cake.

Three quarters of a cup of butter one & a
quarter of sugar, yolks of 6 eggs, half a
cup. of milk, one & a half cups of flour,
sifted, one teaspoonful of baking powder
orange colouring. Proceed in the same
way, with the mixing as in the above
recipe for almond cake. Put half
the mixture into a sandwich tin. &
into the remaining half put a few
drops of orange colouring. Bake in a
good hot oven.

Buns.

Mix together one pound of flour six oz
of butter two teaspoons of baking powder

The original recipe for Mother's Orange Cake (recipe page 110, photographed on page 103)

Glossary

*Items marked * can be obtained from most Indian shops or some supermarkets.*

Aloo	Potato
Atta	Brown whole wheat flour
Bringal	Aubergine
Chittack	2 ounces
Coral	Carom seeds
Dhannia	Coriander
Dhal	Lentils
Garam Masala	Hot Spice*
Ghee	Refined butter (in most cases oil can be used)*
Gill	¼ pint
Jagry	Refined sugar*
Jeera	Cumin seeds*
Jhal Frazee	Hot fry
Jharam	A cloth, usually muslin to strain through
Junket	Soured cream or yogurt
Karti Kebab	Spicy or hot kebab
Koftas	Spicy and hot mince meat balls
Karellas (Kurelas)	A vegetable – bitter gourd or bitter melon. Said to have medicinal properties for diabetes and other illnesses
Kussundi	Kind of pickle
Mattar	Peas
Methe	Fenugreek seeds
Panch-Poran	Five spice*
Paneer	Indian soft cheese*
Plantain	Form of banana
Prawn Balichow	Kind of prawn pickle
Seer	2 pounds
Soojee	Nearest is semolina
Suji	Nearest is semolina
Sujee	Nearest is semolina
Tyre	Soured cream or yogurt

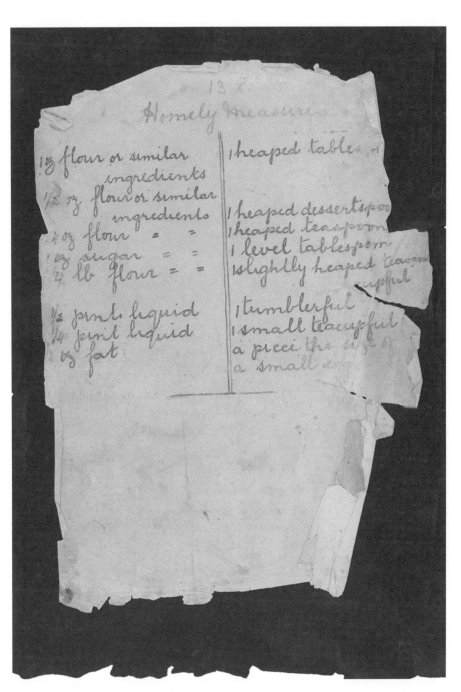

Homely Measures

1 oz flour or similar ingredients	1 heaped tables...
½ oz flour or similar ingredients	
? oz flour = =	1 heaped dessertspoo...
? oz sugar = =	1 heaped teaspoon
¼ lb flour = =	1 level tablespoon
	slightly heaped teaspoo...
	...upful
½ pints liquid	1 tumblerful
¼ pint liquid	1 small teacupful
? oz fat	a piece the size of
	a small e...

Grandmother's definition of 'Homely Measures' from page 138 of her recipe book

Recipe Index

Maureen Forrest, Founder of The Hope Foundation with children who benefit from
The Hope Foundation's projects

ACKNOWLEDGEMENTS

The Publisher and The Hope Foundation would like to thank the following companies and individuals for their generous pro bono involvement and sponsorship which made this book possible:

Brandpoint Design Ltd, for design and artwork
Tony Briscoe Food Photography for shooting the recipe photographs
Penny Stephens, Food Stylist for styling the recipe photographs
Topham Street for providing the recipe photography props
Green Saffron Spices Ltd, for sponsoring the print

brandpoint

Penny Stephens